OVER 100 UNIQUE
SCRIPTURE STUDY METHODS
You've Probably Never Tried

CHAS HATHAWAY

CFI
An Imprint of Cedar Fort, Inc.
Springville, Utah

© 2013 Chas Hathaway
All rights reserved.

No part of this book may be reproduced in any form whatsoever, whether by graphic, visual, electronic, film, microfilm, tape recording, or any other means, without prior written permission of the publisher, except in the case of brief passages embodied in critical reviews and articles.

This is not an official publication of The Church of Jesus Christ of Latter-day Saints. The opinions and views expressed herein belong solely to the author and do not necessarily represent the opinions or views of Cedar Fort, Inc. Permission for the use of sources, graphics, and photos is also solely the responsibility of the author.

ISBN 13: 978-1-4621-1181-7

Published by CFI, an imprint of Cedar Fort, Inc., 2373 W. 700 S., Springville, UT 84663
Distributed by Cedar Fort, Inc., www.cedarfort.com

LIBRARY OF CONGRESS CATALOGING-IN-PUBLICATION DATA

Hathaway, Chas, 1979- author.
 Scripture study made awesome / Chas Hathaway.
   pages cm
 ISBN 978-1-4621-1181-7 (alk. paper)
 1. Church of Jesus Christ of Latter-day Saints--Sacred books--Study and teaching.
 2. Mormon Church--Sacred books--Study and teaching. 3. Church of Jesus
 Christ of Latter-day Saints--Doctrines--Study and teaching. 4. Mormon Church--
 Doctrines--Study and teaching. I. Title.

 BX8622.H38 2013
 289.3'2--dc23

2013007036

Cover design by Rebecca J. Greenwood
Cover design © 2013 by Lyle Mortimer
Edited by Heather Holm

Printed in the United States of America

10 9 8 7 6 5 4 3 2 1

Printed on acid-free paper

Dedication

To Brother Kendall Ayres,
my institute teacher, for helping me see
how awesome the scriptures can be.

Contents

CHAPTER 1: The Scriptures Are Awesome • 1
CHAPTER 2: Getting the Motivation to Just Do It! • 7
CHAPTER 3: Study Medium, Study Sources, Marking Methods, and Study Methods • 19
CHAPTER 4: List of Study Mediums • 23
CHAPTER 5: List of Study Sources • 29
CHAPTER 6: Marking Methods • 35
CHAPTER 7: Semi-Traditional Methods • 43
CHAPTER 8: Marathon Methods • 53
CHAPTER 9: Self-Discovery Methods • 57
CHAPTER 10: Q & A Methods • 69
CHAPTER 11: Deep Study Methods •75
CHAPTER 12: Creative Methods • 107
CHAPTER 13: Family Scripture Study Methods • 125

CONTENTS

CHAPTER 14: Which Methods Will Work Best for Me? • 135

CHAPTER 15: When and How Long to Study • 141

CHAPTER 16: What's So Special about the Book of Mormon? • 149

CHAPTER 17: Family Study • 159

CHAPTER 18: Scripture Study and Revelation • 165

CONCLUSION An Old Treasure • 173

ABOUT THE AUTHOR Chas Hathaway • 181

CHAPTER 1

The Scriptures Are Awesome

> And upon these I write the things of my soul, and many of the scriptures which are engraven upon the plates of brass. For my soul delighteth in the scriptures, and my heart pondereth them, and writeth them for the learning and the profit of my children.
>
> Behold, my soul delighteth in the things of the Lord; and my heart pondereth continually upon the things which I have seen and heard. (2 Nephi 4:15–16)

We all know the scriptures are awesome, but we don't always feel awesome about studying them, especially when we read them so often at church, in meetings, and in our personal and family scripture study. Yet, once in awhile, we experience moments when the scriptures are opened to us in a way that keeps us wanting to study, either because we read something we really need to hear, or because we are touched by the influence of the Spirit. Elder Neal A. Maxwell spoke of such experiences when he said,

> For my part, I am glad the book [of Mormon] will be with us "as long as the earth shall stand." I need and want additional time. For me, [the Book of Mormon is like a vast mansion with] towers, courtyards, and wings [that] await my inspection. My tour of it has never been completed. Some rooms I have yet to enter, and there are more flaming fireplaces waiting to warm me. Even the rooms I have glimpsed contained further furnishings and rich detail yet to be savored. There are panels inlaid with incredible insights, and design and décor dating from Eden. There are also sumptuous banquet tables painstakingly prepared by predecessors, which await all of us. Yet we as church members sometimes behave like hurried tourists, scarcely venturing beyond the entry hall. May we come to feel as a whole people beckoned beyond the entry hall.[1]

Maybe you've felt something similar while

SCRIPTURE STUDY *Made Awesome*

reading the scriptures—that gentle yet powerful influence of the Spirit, or that blast of insight on a verse you've read a billion times; that thirst to keep reading and reading while studying the revelations. But if you're like me, you've asked yourself many times, "How can I get that again? What do I need to do to feel that strong influence of the Spirit every time I read?"

Well, I have some good news, and some bad news. The bad news is, you won't have that experience every time you read. I don't know of anyone who has an "awesome" experience every time. The good news is, you can experience it a whole lot more than you do now, and if you're diligent and work hard at it, you can have awesome scripture study experiences more often than not.

So, how do you do it? Well, that's the purpose of this book. Obviously it won't help the blatantly lazy . . . much. Okay, maybe a little. But what this book will do is allow those willing to engage in active scripture study to never get bored of studying again. Keep this book near your desk and refer to it every time you feel a little blah about studying. Guaranteed, you'll find an approach to scripture study that sounds interesting right now.

CRIMINAL MOTIVATION

Did you know there have been criminals who have experienced conversion from "bumping into" the scriptures? Check this action out. This story was shared by President James E. Faust in general conference. A member of the Church in Puerto Rico set out to give a Book of Mormon to her friend as a gift, so she wrapped it up and put it in her purse. On the way to deliver it, she was attacked by someone who stole her purse with the Book of Mormon inside. Within a few days, she received this letter:

Mrs. Cruz:

> Forgive me, forgive me. You will never know how sorry I am for attacking you. But because of it, my life has changed and will continue to change. That book [the Book of Mormon] has helped me in my life. The dream of that man of God has shaken me. . . . I am returning your five pesos for I can't spend them.

I want you to know that you seemed to have a radiance about you. That light seemed to stop me [from harming you, so] I ran away instead.

I want you to know that you will see me again, but when you do, you won't recognize me, for I will be your brother. . . . Here, where I live, I have to find the Lord and go to the church you belong to.

The message you wrote in that book brought tears to my eyes. Since Wednesday night I have not been able to stop reading it. I have prayed and asked God to forgive me, [and] I ask you to forgive me. . . . I thought your wrapped gift was something I could sell. [Instead,] it has made me want to make my life over. Forgive me, forgive me, I beg you.

Your absent friend.[2]

If the scriptures have power to soften the heart of a hardened criminal, how much more power they must have to change the heart of those who actually want to be touched and changed by them.

If you're willing to do as President Gordon B. Hinckley said and "Take advantage of every opportunity to enlarge your understanding of the gospel,"[3] then you'll find truth in Richard G. Scott's counsel that

> Scriptures can calm an agitated soul, giving peace, hope, and a restoration of confidence in one's ability to overcome the challenges of life. They have potent power to heal emotional challenges when there is faith in the Savior. They can accelerate physical healing.
>
> A scripture that we may have read many times can take on nuances of meaning that are refreshing and insightful when we face a new challenge in life.[4]

Awesome. So let's get started.

NOTES

1. Neal A. Maxwell, *The Great Answer to the Great Question*, FARMS, audio cassette, Deseret Book.

2. James E. Faust, "What I Want My Son to Know before He Leaves on His Mission," *Ensign*, May 1996, 40.

3. Gordon B. Hinckley, "Tithing: An Opportunity to Prove Our Faithfulness," *Ensign*, May 1982, 40.

4. Richard G. Scott, "The Power of Scripture," *Ensign*, November 2011, 6–8.

CHAPTER 2

Getting the Motivation to Just Do It!

For many, the biggest challenge with reading scriptures is having the motivation to want to study. If this is you, I'd like to encourage you to set that aside for ten seconds and do one thing: Regardless of your situation, make the unequivocal, eternally vigilant decision that regardless of how you feel at the moment, promise yourself and God that you will read the scriptures every day for the rest of your life—no exceptions. Exercise whatever willpower it takes and make that decision once for the rest of your life. None of this, "If I miss a day, then . . . ," because you won't miss a day. You will read every day.

Have you done it yet? Stop now, pray, and

make that promise. I'm serious. Stop reading and make that decision before continuing on.

Did you do it? Promise? I mean it. We'll get to motivation in a second. Stop and make that promise to yourself and God. Just do it, right now. I'll wait.

Okay, now we can go on.

Now that you have sworn to yourself and God that you will never again miss another day of scripture study, we can move on to talk about getting the motivation you need. Believe me, the decision you just made is a major part of opening the doors to motivation. Why? Because you no longer have an option. You have to. You're enslaved to the commitment you just made. Motivation makes no difference. Now you can deal with making the best of each situation.

Take a deep breath and congratulate yourself. You're 90 percent of the way there. Now you must work on your attitude toward what is inevitable.

Humans are resilient and pretty good at getting themselves out of bondage, but they are

SCRIPTURE STUDY *Made Awesome*

absolutely phenomenal at making the best of situations they are forced to be in.

You have a powerful built-in need and ability to adapt, and you can make seemingly negative situations prove positive. That's why I asked you to make a commitment first. You can't get out of it, so now you can work on making the best of it.

Joseph B. Wirthlin said,

> Every one of you can read something in the scriptures each day. You should spend some time pondering and studying the scriptures. It is better to read and ponder even one verse than none at all. I challenge each young man [or woman] to read something in the scriptures every day for the rest of your lives. Few things you do will bring you greater dividends.[1]

If you do only read a verse or two a day, make sure you don't skip out on the opportunity of making it a spiritually fulfilling study. President Howard W. Hunter said it this way:

> Reading habits vary widely. There are rapid readers and slow readers, some who read only small snatches at a time and others who persist without stopping until the book is finished. Those who

> delve into the scriptural library, however, find that to understand requires more than casual reading or perusal—there must be concentrated study. It is certain that one who studies the scriptures every day accomplishes far more than one who devotes considerable time one day and then lets days go by before continuing. . . . The important thing is to allow nothing else to ever interfere with our study.[2]

If you ever find yourself trying to decide whether you should read right now, then stop and tell yourself, "Don't think about it. Just do it."

> The Church must be cleansed, and I proclaim against all iniquity. A man is saved no faster than he gets knowledge, for if he does not get knowledge, he will be brought into captivity by some evil power in the other world, as evil spirits will have more knowledge, and consequently more power than many men who are on the earth. Hence it needs revelation to assist us, and give us knowledge of the things of God.[3]

The thing that will kill your resolve faster than anything is procrastination. Once you've made your decision to read every day, then start reading. Start today. Start now. If you've been away from the scriptures for a while, put this

SCRIPTURE STUDY *Made Awesome*

book down, read a chapter from the scriptures, and then come back to this book.

When I first got engaged to Jenni, we were talking about our determination to read together as a family every day.

I thought I was so smart to enthusiastically say, "In fact, I suggest we start reading together the day we get married!"

But Jenni taught me a great lesson with her simple response. "Why not today?"

So we read together that day, and the next. From then on, any day we were together, our activities included at least a short scripture study.

Don't wait. Start now.

And yes, we even read on our wedding day.

MOTIVATION-BUILDING IDEAS
PRAY

I know this is an obvious one, but there's a reason for that. God is real. He wants to speak with you, even if you don't feel like talking to Him. Talk to Him and ask Him to help you want to study. Even more important, ask Him to help you enjoy your study when you do it. He really is pleased with your commitment to study every day. One of the ways He might reward your decision is by giving you a better experience doing it.

Make sure that you begin your study with prayer. This will help get your mind into a spiritual mood and bridge your thoughts from whatever you were doing to what you're about to do.

SLOW DOWN

One of the reasons people tend to dread study is that it's a slow-paced activity. We live in a society that thrives on fast-paced, multitasking explosions of activity, noise, play, and motion. Going from rushed normal activity to a slow, contemplative activity can seem daunting. If it's almost time to study and you don't feel like it, try taking a walk or sitting and listening to soft, enjoyable music for five minutes. A slow, pleasant activity will allow your mind to ease into a ponderous mood. This is another way that prayer can help. Feel free to mix any of these—pray while walking or listening to soft music, or take a short casual drive while saying a prayer in your heart. Art, yoga, or gentle exercise will also work—anything that slows your mind enough to prepare for study.

THINK OF STUDY AS "ME TIME"

Our society is obsessed with "me time," probably because of the "I've been doing so much for everyone else that I just need a break" syndrome. Reading scriptures is a chance to recharge and can be compared to "sharpening the saw," which is this:

Imagine you are busy sawing a log. I come and say, "You know, that saw is dull. You'd be able to cut more wood faster if you stopped to sharpen the saw."

You look up and reply, "I don't have time to sharpen the saw, I'm too busy cutting wood."

Some say that "me time" is a form of sharpening the saw. I sometimes agree with this; however, some use "me time" as an excuse to get out of their duties. They feel they have a right to play and put off important things for a while. There's great danger in that, especially when family or church duties are neglected for sub-wholesome recreation. But if you can use scripture study as "me time" and decide that it's rejuvenating, then your mind will start looking forward to it.

POSITIVE REINFORCEMENT

Reward yourself. Every week that you keep your resolution to study every day, you deserve a treat. That might be a goodie, the opportunity to go to a favorite store, or to play a favorite game. Do this as long as it takes to convince your mind to look forward to scripture study. Associating scripture study with something your heart or mind already crave will promote a love for it.

LEARN WHAT MAKES YOU TICK

Get to know yourself well enough to understand your motivations. Why do you prefer certain things over others? Why do you approach situations the way you do? Sometimes taking personality profile and other psychological quizzes can help you quantify and recognize why you do what you do. Once you feel that you have a grasp on your true motivations and desires, use that knowledge to enhance your scripture study.

MAKING THE TIME

Sometimes the hardest part about learning to do something habitually is finding time to make it happen. Habits don't come automatically, but the mere act of doing something every day will help form the desired habit. If you are someone who can't seem to find the time no matter what you try, consider some of the following ideas:

GET UP TEN MINUTES EARLIER: You can afford ten minutes. For this? Yes. Seriously, you can afford ten minutes.

GO TO BED TEN MINUTES LATER: If getting up early doesn't work, try staying up ten minutes later. One of these suggestions should solve the time issue—really. Dropping your sleep time from six hours per night to five hours, fifty minutes will actually be of great benefit to you if it means getting in scripture study every day. The study doesn't have to be effective all the time; it just has to be there. People have died by doing things out of sheer determination. We're human beings. We have power over our own minds and bodies. We can make things happen.

Make *this* happen!

And by the way, I don't think ten minutes of study per day will kill you.

PUT THE BABY DOWN FOR TEN MINUTES: I know this can be difficult, even agonizing for young mothers, but devoting ten minutes to God will do far more to bless your children than you realize. If you have toddlers, you might need to lock them in their room for ten minutes. Tell them what it's for, and then force yourself to ignore the bangs and wails that come from the bedroom. It's only for ten minutes. They'll survive, especially since the Lord wants you to take that time.

If you can find a way to make it work, you could even try reading with them, as long as they don't stop you from studying or distract you from what you're trying to do.

LISTEN TO THE SCRIPTURES DURING YOUR COMMUTE: We'll talk more about listening to audio scriptures later, but if you have a ten minute commute each day, get a CD or MP3 player and play ten minutes of scriptures in the car. Believe it or not, that's about an average chapter length in audio scriptures. Even if your car has no audio hookups (which most do), put batteries in your player. If this is the only possible time you can make for scripture study, you can find a way to make it work.

BE CREATIVE: Human beings are naturally creative. Use that creativity to carve ten minutes out of a ridiculous schedule. If you find that your plate is too full for scripture study, you need to get rid of something in your life. I don't care who you are. You can, and you should. You can make time for God.

Harold B. Lee warned that,

> Testimony isn't something you have today, and you are going to have always. A testimony is fragile. It is as hard to hold as a moonbeam. It is something you have to recapture every day of your life.[4]

So how do we rekindle that testimony every day? By studying the scriptures daily. They aren't a one-time discovery. We can rediscover the scriptures regularly. Spencer W. Kimball once said,

> I am convinced that each of us, at some time in our lives, must discover the scriptures for ourselves—and not just discover them once, but rediscover them again and again.[5]

For the rest of you, let's talk about making your scripture time more fun and fulfilling.

NOTES

1. Joseph B. Wirthlin, "Growing into the Priesthood," *Ensign*, November 1999, 38.

2. Howard W. Hunter, "Reading the Scriptures," *Ensign*, November 1979, 64.

3. Joseph Smith, *Teachings of the Prophet Joseph Smith*, Selected by Joseph Fielding Smith (Salt Lake City: Deseret Book, 1976), 217.

4. Harold B. Lee, "President Harold B. Lee Directs Church; Led By the Spirit," *Church News*, July 15, 1972, 4.

5. Spencer W. Kimball, "How Rare a Possession—the Scriptures!" *Ensign*, September 1976, 4–5.

CHAPTER 3

Study Medium, Study Sources, Marking Methods, and Study Methods

In order to avoid confusion, I'm going to differentiate the terms *study medium, study sources, marking methods, and study methods.*

STUDY MEDIUM

The type of medium we will refer to in this book is any medium that is used as an instrument of study. This could be a book, a notebook, a computer, or anything else that can hold information. In basic terms, we are referring to any device, electronic or otherwise, that is used to help us study.

STUDY SOURCES

A study source is the specific media being studied. The standard works are a source (regardless of whether they are in book form, audio, video, or whatever). General conference is a source. The hymns are a source. We'll list appropriate gospel study sources in a later chapter.

MARKING METHODS

A marking method is a technique used to place emphasis on a verse, a word, a phrase, or a quote. Marking implies doing something to the page or text to make it stand out, such as underlining, italicizing, color-coding, or highlighting. I differentiate this from study methods, because many study methods include marking. However, the actual marking method (whether you color, circle, underline, or bracket) does not matter.

STUDY METHODS

A study method is a technique for studying. Reading chronologically is a study method. So is searching for key words or painting while listening to audio scriptures. Listing various unique study methods is the primary focus of this book.

CHAPTER 4

List of Study Mediums

This list is not intended to be comprehensive. It is to help you recognize the different mediums you have at your disposal. Most likely you have a set of scriptures, and most likely you have access to a pen. What other means might you use in your study?

BOOKS

This is probably the most obvious study medium. Leather-bound, hardback, or paperback scriptures are major study mediums, but they aren't the only ones. Scriptural commentaries and books by general authorities are also study mediums.

NOTEBOOK

Using a notebook (paper or digital) in your study can really open your eyes and bring out new insights. There are so many methods involving a notebook that it must be considered its own medium. I've heard it said that in the classroom, the ultimate visual aid is the chalkboard. A notebook can be your personal chalkboard. On it you can write, draw, map, transcribe, translate, diagram, record, analyze, break up, break down, break dance—okay, maybe not break dance—examine, quote, and cartoonify anything you encounter in your study.

JOURNAL

This is similar to the notebook, but it implies a permanent record, meaning that it's intended to be kept and passed on to posterity. I suggest that whenever you record personal thoughts, feelings, ideas, or experiences, you use some kind of journal instead of just a notebook. You might want to have a personal journal and a scripture journal. Or, if you're like me, you could use a text document that allows you to have both in separate sections of the same document.

COMPUTER

This is a big one. It's like a notebook times one billion. Or, to put it another way, it's like a notebook with unlimited pages and information that you can cut, paste, and organize indefinitely. You can also include maps, photos, entire chapters, Internet links, and thoughts, which can turn your personal scripture study notebook into a full-length volume of scriptural commentary. It might sound intimidating to approach study with that in mind, but just imagine how big a book would be if every thought, marking, cross reference, and lesson that you personally have had, made, or attended in your life were recorded in it. Most likely, it would look something like a twenty-six-volume Encyclopedia Britannica. With a computer, you have the ability to start recording now. Back them up and/or print them out, and they'll last forever. What a great thing to share with your great-grandchildren—and beyond!

INTERNET

Some might lump Internet in with computer, but there is power in the cloud! Consider it the international collection of stored information.

You obviously have to be careful with this medium so you don't bump into the wrong "information" or get confused by someone's personal commentary. Nevertheless, there are so many incredible sources, as well as so many means to record, share, document, and engage in your own study that it would be foolish to disregard it.

MOBILE DEVICE

Some might lump mobile devices with Internet, but consider the convenience and accessibility your mobile device gives the Internet. You can take and use photos (or a video) of religious material to paste (or link to) in your scripture notebook. You can record audio of thoughts and questions. You can share what you discover in your study with friends on social networks. The possibilities are endless.

AUDIO SCRIPTURES

Between scriptures on MP3, Internet audio, CD, DVD, and cassettes (I know—*so* 1985!), audio versions of the scriptures are available to virtually everyone. We'll talk about the advantages and disadvantages of audio as we go along, but audio scriptures open an entire new universe of scripture study methods. We may include with this medium audio conference, audio Church magazines, audio manuals, and the audio of any other modern-day scripture.

YOUR OWN MIND

You probably haven't even considered this one, but your own mind can be a medium. Many of the methods discussed in this book will require thinking, pondering, reviewing, memorizing, or imagining. Your mind is a major study medium, and it's the only one that is consistently needed with all the others. It's also the only one that can be used independent of the others.

PRAYER

I don't think it takes much to convince you that prayer is a necessary part of studying. It's the medium used most by the prophets, and it's generally used (and should *always* be used) in addition to whatever other medium you are using for study.

CHAPTER 5

List of Study Sources

Listing all the things you can use for scripture study would take a long time, but here are a some common ones you might want to consider.

STANDARD WORKS

The standard works are obviously the most important and most common study source. These come in physical formats, digital formats, audio formats, and even video formats. And if you're a good memorizer, they can come in mental formats, too, but all are the same basic source.

GENERAL CONFERENCE MESSAGES

This ought to be next on our list in order of importance. We should study the words of living prophets at least as diligently as we study the standard works. They represent God's words to us now. They also come in all of the formats that the standard works come in, with one addition: live format!

OTHER TALKS BY PROPHETS AND GENERAL AUTHORITIES

Between firesides, BYU speeches, seminary morningsides, and travel visits by general authorities, there is quite a collection of other official words by modern prophets. These can be great resources for gospel study, and many can be found on the Internet.

BOOKS BY PROPHETS AND GENERAL AUTHORITIES

There might be fewer of these than those previously mentioned, but there are still more of them than the average person can read in a lifetime. Check your local LDS bookstore or your parents' study. They're out there!

OFFICIAL CHURCH MANUALS

These can include gospel doctrine, priesthood, and Relief Society manuals; institute (one of my personal favorites), seminary, Primary, and

Sunday School manuals; and a plethora of manuals that the Church continually publishes. My rule of thumb is that if you can find it at the distribution center, it's probably good gospel study material. Even the children's scripture readers can have good commentary on chapters, verses, and historical events in the standard works that are hard to understand. Obviously most of these sources should not replace the standard works, but many of them can help you get more out of your scripture study and the words of the living prophets.

THE HYMNS

The hymns of the Church were chosen carefully to reflect the Spirit and doctrine of the gospel of Jesus Christ, and some even call the hymnbook their "green scriptures." While it doesn't replace the scriptures, the hymnbook is still a great resource for obtaining the Spirit of the Lord, and using it during scripture study can be beneficial.

THE OFFICIAL HISTORY OF THE CHURCH

The History of the Church, recorded by Joseph Smith and compiled by B. H. Roberts, is a strong testimony of the Latter-day work of the Lord. It is regularly referenced in the Doctrine and Covenants. Reading and using it as a study guide gives the student a broader view of the gospel message, especially in regard to the Restoration in these last days. If you dig a bit, you can even find it online.

YOUR PATRIARCHAL BLESSING

I once heard Thomas S. Monson say, "Your patriarchal blessing is to you a personal Liahona to chart your course and guide your way."[1] Studying your patriarchal blessing regularly and often is important and ranks as one of the most important things to include in your gospel study.

JOURNALS

Your journal can be a powerful testament to the Lord's hand in your life, not just in reading it, but also in writing it. In addition, the journals of your ancestors can help solidify your testimony as you see the effects of the gospel in their lives. Those ancestors who were not religious can be quiet testaments of how the Lord led them to where they needed to be so that you and your family could receive the gospel.

CHURCH MAGAZINES

The Church magazines, such as the *Ensign,* the *Liahona,* the *New Era,* and the *Children's Friend,* offer the Lord's word to us for our time today. We receive them more often than general conference. The first presidency message and the instruction given by the Apostles and general women leaders are especially worth studying.

Now that we've discussed medium and sources, let's talk about marking ideas.

NOTES

1. Thomas S. Monson, "Your Patriarchal Blessing: A Liahona of Light," *Ensign*, November 1986, 65–67.

CHAPTER 6

Marking Methods

When it comes to scripture marking, Elder Boyd K. Packer is one of my heroes. His scriptures are loaded with margin notes, highlights, and underlines. He was once in Florida with President Gordon B. Hinckley. When President Hinckley was speaking, he turned back to Elder Packer and asked him if he could borrow his scriptures. Elder Packer handed them to President Hinckley, who flipped through them for a few seconds. Then he turned back and said, "I can't read this. You have everything crossed out!"[1]

I suppose underlining is the most common marking method, but there are dozens of other ways to mark the scriptures. If you're using more than one study method that involves marking, then you might want to use more than one marking method so you don't get confused when you read the verse again later. If this is what you decide to do, then you might want to create a "key" in the front or back cover to help you keep track of what the different markings represent. Consistency will help future study.

If you're not concerned about being able to identify your markings, that's okay too, as long as you decide ahead of time that it's the initial study that matters most to you.

You also might want to test your writing utensils to make sure that none of them will bleed through the pages of your scriptures.

Now let's discuss some marking methods. Keep in mind that most of these techniques can be used in both digital and analog versions of the standard works.

MARKING METHOD IDEAS

UNDERLINING: The old standby; however, there are ways to make the old standby more diverse, such as using different colors or different utensils (pens, pencils, markers, colored pencils, or crayons—yes, I've even seen crayons).

BRACKETS: Brackets are these things: [ ]. They're like a box, minus the top and bottom—if that makes sense. Many students of the scriptures like brackets, because they don't cover the text. You can bracket individual words, entire verses, or entire pages.

BOXES AND CIRCLES: You can draw a box around a verse, or you can circle it. You can also box or circle individual words or phrases. Or you can use both marking methods. As an example, boxed scriptures can represent those that relate to your calling, and circled scriptures can be those that relate to your family. You can use dotted lines, boxes, brackets, or circles to represent other things.

ASTERISKS, LETTERS, AND OTHER SYMBOLS: Don't forget smiley faces, the star of David, or even the trademark sign. You can use a big SM next to scripture masteries, or a single M next to missionary verses. You can have individual letters or groups of letters (or characters) to represent different things.

CREATE A COLOR CODE: This is a method that can expand the others. What does the green star mean? What about the red star? Blue underline? Yellow underline?

NUMBERING: This technique borderlines on being a study method, but since there are so many different things you can number, it can also be a marking method. You can number items in a scriptural list, count the number of times a word or name is used, or rate scriptures by number. Numbering can be a good way to put an order to things or show the relationship of different things within the verses. They can also be used for customized footnoting.

DRAWING CONNECTORS: When you find verses or words on a page that can add insight by linking them together, mark them both (circle, bracket, or whatever) and draw a connecting line from one to another. This works to make scriptural lists, make if/then connections, clarify genealogies, keep context straight, make diagrams, and dozens of other things.

BACKGROUND COLOR CODE: If you're on a computer, you can change the background color of text (as opposed to changing the color of the text itself). This is similar to highlighting, which you can also do on a computer.

KEEP A NOTEBOOK: This is also a medium, but you can mark verses, phrases, or words by copying them into a notebook, a document, an email, or a 3 x 5 card.

BOLD, ITALICS, AND BOLD ITALICS: You must be careful when using italics on computer scriptures, because some verses in the Bible already have italicized words. The italicized words in the King James Bible were added by the translators to help the reader. The added words were necessary, because word meanings and idioms change when a book is translated. To make sure that everyone understood that these words were not in the available manuscript, the translators set them in italics.[2] Using bold and bold italics should be safe, however. Either one will work in marking quotes from conference or other scriptures or articles.

As an example of how you might use various marking methods, you might use red underlining to draw attention to the words of the Savior, red brackets to draw attention to scriptures that help you when you are teaching, and green circles to emphasize examples of exercising faith. There is no limit to how many ways you can mark your scriptures. The trick is to use the ones you are most comfortable with and like the best.

GO HIGHLIGHT HAPPY

If you want to have a little fun with marking, try taking it to the extreme. If you're an organization ogre, a detail demon, or a labeling . . . uh . . . llama, you might like to try several study methods that involve marking and implement them all.

Get one of those cool four-color pens, or a bouquet of new colored pencils with a four-pack of highlighters. Mark scripture masteries with a red box, missionary verses with a blue box, verses dealing with family matters with a black box, and favorite scriptures with a green box.

Use red underline for doctrinal verses, green for promise scriptures, black for warnings, and blue for commandments. Then use red asterisks for "know" scriptures, green for "feel" verses, black for "do" scriptures, and so on. Whatever things are worth marking, pick a marking medium and a color for each one. Don't forget the smiley faces, stars, stick men, strikethroughs, and highlights.

I once had about twenty-five codes to use for marking. Of course, after awhile I lost track of which was which, even with the key I put in the back, but it sure made for some fun marking. Plus my old set of scriptures looked like a party.

The precise marking method you use doesn't matter nearly as much as the opportunity marking gives you to personally interact with the scriptures. So figure out what works best for you and make it fun.

NOTES

1. Boyd K. Packer, "The Book of Mormon: Another Testament of Jesus Christ," *Ensign*, November 2001, 62.
2. See http://www.biblebelievers.com/jmelton/italics.html.

CHAPTER 7

Semi-Traditional Methods

We'll soon talk about unique, creative methods of study that most people haven't tried, but first we'll consider the old standbys, since they've been tried and tested and, for a lot of good reasons, are still standing the test of time.

STUDY REFERENCES FROM A FAVORITE TALK

If you have a favorite talk, whether from the most recent conference, an *Ensign*, or a book or website, use it as a basis for a few study sessions. Find all the scriptures referenced in the talk and read them. Read the verses around them, and study the footnotes.

FIND TALKS ABOUT A FAVORITE SCRIPTURE

When you get to a verse you like, look up all the conference talks you can find that mention that verse. A fabulous resource for this is online: http://scriptures/byu.edu.

They've created a database of talks that mention verses of scripture throughout the standard works. But if you want to build your own similar database, or just read talks about the verse, go to the LDS.org website and search for words from the verse. For example, if you type "I will go and do," with the quotation marks in place, you'll probably be given a dozen talks that mention the verse. Study those talks and find more scriptures from them.

IF/THEN

The scriptures are filled with if/then statements, although the words "if" and "then" don't always appear. They are the verses that teach that *if* such is the case, *then* such will happen. Here are some examples:

> 20 And inasmuch as [if] ye shall keep my commandments, [then] ye shall prosper, and shall be led to a land of promise; yea, even a land which I have prepared for you; yea, a land which is choice above all other lands.

SCRIPTURE STUDY *Made Awesome*

21 And inasmuch as [if] thy brethren shall rebel against thee, [then] they shall be cut off from the presence of the Lord.

22 And inasmuch as [if] thou shalt keep my commandments, [then] thou shalt be made a ruler and a teacher over thy brethren.

23 For behold, in that day that they [if] shall rebel against me, [then] I will curse them even with a sore curse, and they shall have no power over thy seed except they shall rebel against me also.

24 And if it so be that they rebel against me, [then] they shall be a scourge unto thy seed, to stir them up in the ways of remembrance. (1 Nephi 2:20–24)

Look for if/then scriptures and see how many you can find. Chances are, if you look close, you'll be able to find at least two or three per page, and probably more. Mark the *if* and *then* and draw a line from one to the other to note the connection.

COLOR-CODE THE FOOTNOTES

Look for footnotes in the scriptures that have alternate translations, such as Hebrew, Greek, or

Joseph Smith Translation. Pick a color to represent each and mark both the footnote at the bottom of the page and the word in the verse. Don't forget to mark the IEs (in explanations) too! Then, when you come back later and read it again, you will see the quick, simple explanations.

TAKE NOTES

Turn on some audio scriptures and take notes. You can either listen for something specific, or just write as much as possible of what you hear. The idea is not to get it *all* down, but to try to get as much down as possible, because as you do, your concentration will grow stronger. You can either write by hand or type, but see how much you can catch.

Bruce R. McConkie said the following:

> Perhaps the perfect pattern . . . is to teach what is found in the scriptures and then to put a seal of living reality upon it by telling a similar and equivalent thing that has happened in our dispensation and to our people and—most ideally—to us as individuals.[1]

SCRIPTURE STUDY *Made Awesome*

ASK WHY IT WAS WRITTEN

Elder L. Tom Perry gave a great study method suggestion when he said,

> Each time we read the book [of Mormon] we should probably ask ourselves: "Why did these writers choose these particular stories or events to include in the record? What value are they for us today?"[2]

As you read the scriptures, consider this question and write your thoughts in your scripture journal.

WHITEBOARD THE EVENTS AS YOU LISTEN

Use your notebook as a whiteboard and write or map out what's happening in the verses. This works especially well if you listen to the scriptures instead of reading them so that your eyes and hands are free to write and draw.

RANDOM RELATEDNESS

Flip the scriptures open to a random spot, and then, while holding that spot, flip to another. Read the two verses and try to find ways that they are related. If the answer comes easy, try again. If it's hard, dig deeper. *Somehow* the doctrine or concepts are related.

LOVE NOTES

My wife introduced me to "love notes," although I think everyone's familiar with them. Open your scriptures believing that the first thing you read is a love note from your Heavenly Father.

Jenni's experience with this method demonstrates its potential. She was in seminary as a teenager when her teacher told the class about love notes. The idea immediately caught on, and the students were sharing their great experiences about opening the scriptures and finding just the right message for their situation at the time.

Jenni tried it, but it didn't seem to work. She attempted it several times, but the verses just didn't seem to speak to her—until about her tenth try. She opened her scriptures to Helaman 5:12, which says,

> And now, my sons, remember, remember that it is upon the rock of our Redeemer, who is Christ, the Son of God, that ye must build your foundation; that when the devil shall send forth his mighty winds, yea, his shafts in the whirlwind, yea, when all his hail and his mighty storm shall beat upon you, it shall have no power over you to drag you down to the gulf of misery and endless wo, because of the rock upon

which ye are built, which is a sure foundation, a foundation whereon if men build they cannot fall.

That verse stood out to her so powerfully that it became a love note for her life. She has ever after called it her favorite scripture, as well as her theme. She even made "How Firm a Foundation"[3] her new favorite hymn.

STUDY THE SUNDAY SCHOOL OR PRIESTHOOD/RELIEF SOCIETY LESSON

Revolutionary, eh? It actually makes for a fabulous scripture study! Follow along in the guide and read each of the suggested verses. If you don't have the study guide, find it on LDS.org. It's there . . . I promise.

USE THE BIBLE DICTIONARY

Look up a person, place, or topic in the Bible Dictionary and then read all the scriptures mentioned in the entry. Once you learn all you can find on the subject, try another Bible dictionary entry—perhaps one from something you read in the first entry. If you really like the BD, start with the first entry and read through the entire thing. There's some pretty cool stuff in there.

FIND SCRIPTURAL LISTS

The scriptures are loaded with lists. See if you can identify them. It might help to mark the items by number so you'll clearly recognize the list later. As an example:

> Wherefore, the fruit of thy loins shall write; and the fruit of the loins of Judah shall write; and that which shall be written by the fruit of thy loins, and also that which shall be written by the fruit of the loins of Judah, shall grow together, unto the [1] confounding of false doctrines and [2] laying down of contentions, and [3] establishing peace among the fruit of thy loins, and [4] bringing them to the knowledge of their fathers in the latter days, and also to the [5] knowledge of my covenants, saith the Lord. (See 2 Nephi 3:12.)

Scriptural lists are fun to look for and help quantify doctrines and teachings. See how many you can find during your study.

REPLACE SCRIPTURAL NAMES WITH YOUR NAME

We are encouraged to liken the scriptures to ourselves, and one of the ways you can remember to do this is to use your name instead of scriptural names. If the scripture says, "Behold I say unto my servant, Oliver . . . ," change Oliver to your name. Then consider what the Lord is telling *you*.

You can also do it with verses that don't address anyone by name, such as:

> And I give unto you [Chas] a commandment that ye shall do these things. And if ye shall always do these things blessed are ye, for ye are built upon my rock. (See 3 Nephi 18:12.)

LOOK FOR VERSES RELATING TO YOUR LIFE SITUATION

Use the scriptures to see how you can improve in your schoolwork, your friendships, your dating, your calling, your marriage, or your parenting. Pick a life topic that has to do with where you are struggling or would like help. Notice the parenting skills of our Father in Heaven and how the Lord deals with His people. Compare how the righteous deal with their children with how the wicked deal with theirs, or how wicked spouses deal with things differently than righteous spouses. If you're not a parent, see what the verse says about being a good son, daughter, brother, sister, or friend.

Instead of going to the Topical Guide, read

straight through the scriptures from the beginning and look for things related to your chosen life topic.

READ ON THE HOUSETOP

The Book of Mormon states that "the day cometh that the words of the book [scriptures] which were sealed shall be read upon the house tops" (2 Nephi 27:11). Why wait? Take your scriptures on your roof, sit, and read. You might find it a nice atmosphere for studying. Or go somewhere else—sometimes just reading in a different setting than what you're used to can open your mind in ways you might not expect.

NOTES

1. Bruce R. McConkie, "The How and Why of Faith-Promoting Stories," *New Era*, July 1978, 4.

2. L. Tom Perry, "Blessings Resulting from Reading the Book of Mormon," *Ensign*, November 2005, 6.

3. *Hymns*, no. 85.

CHAPTER 8

Marathon Methods

The trick with any resolution is to do it, no matter how rotten or tired you feel. This is not about the spiritual benefits. It's about your capacity to do something you choose to, no matter what the difficulty or the consequences might be.

MARATHON 1: BOOK OF MORMON IN A MONTH

If you do well with marathon reading, read the entire Book of Mormon in a month. Or try reading the New Testament in two weeks, or the Old Testament in six months. Or, if you want to do a quadrathlon, read all four standard works in a year. It won't be easy, but if you're a good reader, it's possible.

MARATHON 2: LISTEN TO THE BOOK OF MORMON ONCE A MONTH FOR A YEAR

Quickly listening to the Book of Mormon all the way through actually gives you a lot of interesting insights, so think how much *more* you'll get if you listen to the entire Book of Mormon in a month—twelve times a year!

MARATHON 3: GOSPELS IN A WEEK

Read all four of the New Testament gospels in a week. If that's too short, do a month.

READ THE OLD TESTAMENT IN A MONTH

Read the Old Testament in a month. It's bigger than it looks, but it's also full of gospel gems. Give it a try, especially if you've never read it before. If you come across stories or teachings that confuse you, make a note of it so you can come back to those places next month.

READ ABOUT THE SAVIOR FOR A MONTH

Go to the Topical Guide and look up Jesus Christ and read every verse given about him. Then read through the verses under every subtopic about him. You'll find listings such as

SCRIPTURE STUDY *Made Awesome*

Jesus Christ, Atonement of; Jesus Christ, Advocate; Jesus Christ, Corporeal Nature of; and so on. Now here's the resolution: you only have one month to read every listed verse.

READ EVERY DAY FOR A YEAR

Start at the beginning of the Book of Mormon, and no matter how good or bad your reading has been lately, read a chapter—a *full chapter*—every day. The rule is that you *can't* skip, split the chapter, or miss even one day for an entire year.

LISTEN TO ALL THE CONFERENCES ON LDS.ORG

LDS.org has MP3s of all the general conference sessions back to 1971. Listen to all of them within six months. If you can find the old CDs or cassettes, you might be able to go back even further than that. Keep a notebook handy so that when you hear a quote you really like, jot down three or four words of it verbatim. Then, when you're in a position to look it up online, add quote marks to it and search for it. You'll find the entire quote. Example: "Success can compensate" will get you the full quote, and you can copy it into your study notebook or journal.

CHAPTER 9

Self-Discovery Methods

CROSS-REFERENCE YOUR PATRIARCHAL BLESSING

This is a great way to learn more about yourself and your relationship with your Father in Heaven. You can either make a copy to write on, or type your blessing and store it on your computer. (I recommend doing that anyway!) Then place footnotes or endnotes next to anything that relates back to the scriptures or the words of the living prophets. If you're using a computer, you can include quotes, entire verses of scripture, personal thoughts, and even journal entries.

If you find that you enjoy this method, request copies of the patriarchal blessings of your ancestors from the Church, and cross-reference those, too. Requesting the blessings of dead ancestors is easy: just email PatriarchalBlessing@ldschurch.org and tell them the names and birth dates of your ancestors. Or, you can visit https://apps.lds.org/pbrequest/request/pb-info.jsf and fill out the form provided. Remember to include your member number so they know it's really you, and your address so they can ship it to you. They'll do it!

DO A PERSONALITY PROFILE ON PEOPLE IN THE SCRIPTURES

If you've ever heard of the Hartman personality profile (the color code), or any other personality profile, run it on Nephi, Ammon, Shiz, or any other Book of Mormon character. Do as much studying as necessary to find out what their personalities are.

Or reverse this. You've probably seen the silly Facebook apps "Which Book of Mormon Character Are You?" Instead of settling for a Facebook app, do your own. I don't mean create a profile test; I mean study the people in the scriptures and see which person you are most like. Which one acts most like you? Which one thinks or reacts most like you?

EMULATE A SCRIPTURE HERO

Rather than finding a person in the scriptures who *is* like you, try finding someone you want to be like, and then emulate him or her for a week. Don't pretend to *be* them or act like they would if they were here. Just take some study time getting to know them and then strive to copy their positive traits.

CREATE A TOP-TEN FAVORITE SCRIPTURES LIST

Study to decide on your top ten favorite scriptures. Choosing ten will take a lot of in depth study. Put them in order of most favorite, and spend time considering why certain ones should be higher ranked than others. You might find a lot of self- and scriptural-reflection time.

Another way to approach this is to challenge your favorite scripture. Search the scriptures to see if you can find a verse you like even more. Carefully read your "almost favorite" verses to find some meanings that you might not have noticed before. Find unique applications to yourself in the verses, and see if you can tip the new verse to replace your favorite one.

If you have a hard time thinking of other

verses to compete with your favorite, go to some close family members and friends and ask them for their favorites. Then read their verses to see if there is one of them that has a chance of becoming your favorite.

If that doesn't work, start at the beginning of the Book of Mormon and reread the entire thing. Then go on to the New Testament, Pearl of Great Price, and Doctrine and Covenants. If you still haven't found a new favorite verse, read the Old Testament. If that doesn't do it, you might have to get ideas by reading from old general conference addresses to find the favorite scriptures of the prophets. With each new general conference, listen for new verses to add to your top-ten list.

STUDY YOUR INTERESTS AND HOBBIES

Find out what the scriptures say about your hobbies, interests, and favorite pastimes. If you like gardening, see what you can learn from them about gardening. If you love music, see what they say about that. You'd be surprised how many subjects are at least mentioned in the scriptures. Maybe you're an Internet addict. See

SCRIPTURE STUDY *Made Awesome*

if the scriptures prophesy of the existence of the Internet. (I'll give you a hint: they do!) What do they say about its use?

Although this wouldn't be something you'd want to use as your permanent method, it could make a fun study for a few days, or even weeks, if you really get into it.

Just off the top of my head, I know of verses that touch on such topics such as cooking, dancing, sewing, technology, writing, music, hunting, art, reading, research, athletics—and yes, sleeping. Is your hobby mentioned in the scriptures? Find out!

You can take this to another level if you use the methods of your hobbies to study the scriptures. Not all hobbies have an adaptable method, but some do.

I once heard someone say, "Architecture is frozen music."

As a musician, this idea caught my attention, and I thought to myself, "If that's so, then what would a temple sound like?"

I then spent several months attending the temple and studying the scriptures about the temple and researching the biblical account of temple structure and musical form and instrumentation as it might be used to emulate the temple's architecture. I never built the musical temple that I wish I had time to build, but what a fun study it was!

WHAT WOULD I DO?

Consider how you would react if you were in the same situation taking place in the scriptures you are presently studying. Think honestly and authentically. Knowing yourself as you are now, how would you react if *your* dad said it was time to move into the wilderness? When you feel you know how you would react in that situation, read the next thing that happens and consider how you would react if you were involved in it. Consider yourself in the different roles. How would you react if you were Nephi? How would react if you were Lehi? Sam? Laman? One of the sons of Mosiah? Helaman? Helaman's son? Helaman's dad? How would you honestly react?

SCRIPTURE STUDY *Made Awesome*

MOST CHALLENGING SCRIPTURE LIST

Make a list of the ten scriptures you find most challenging, whether it's because you struggle with the doctrine, they involve your favorite sins, or you just don't understand them. Make that list and resolve to do something about each one. For the doctrinal scriptures, prayerfully study the doctrine until you are comfortable with it. With the favorite sins, resolve to overcome them. And with the confusing scriptures, study and pray to understand them. You might want to use conference talks, scriptural commentary, and a lot of prayer, but it will be well worth the effort. Once you feel comfortable with the topic discussed, or understand it better, rebuild your top-ten most challenging scripture list and repeat the process.

Another way to utilize this method is to look for and make a list of apparent contradictions in the scriptures. Once you find them, study to learn the true doctrine behind the verses and what makes them appear to be contradictory.

I had an interesting experience with this.

I was reading my scriptures at the LDS Institute building one morning when my favorite teacher came up to me and said, "Hey Chas, I have an interesting question, and I'd love to hear your take on it."

"Sure, what is it?"

"A student came to me this morning and pointed out an apparent contradiction in the scriptures, and I'm not sure how to respond."

"What do the verses say?"

He opened his Bible and his Book of Mormon and read,

> There hath no temptation taken you but such as is common to man: but God is faithful, who will not suffer you to be tempted above that ye are able; but will with the temptation also make a way to escape, that ye may be able to bear it. (1 Corinthians 10:13)

"Now that makes it sound like the Lord won't let a person be tempted beyond their ability to resist, right? But here's the other one. He opened his Book of Mormon.

> But that ye would humble yourselves before the Lord, and call on his holy name, and watch and pray continually, that ye may not be tempted above that which ye can bear. (Alma 13:28)

SCRIPTURE STUDY *Made Awesome*

My teacher looked up. "His question is, if Satan can't tempt us beyond our ability to resist, like the scripture in Corinthians says, then why does the scripture in Alma make it sound like it's possible?"

I looked at the two verses. He was right. One verse promised that temptation won't be too strong to resist, and the other warns us about temptation getting too strong to resist.

"Interesting," I said. "Let me study it for a bit, and I'll let you know if I find anything."

My teacher went back to his office, and I looked at the verses over and over. I knew that true revealed scripture never contradicts itself, so that meant there was something we were missing.

> God . . . will not suffer you to be tempted above that ye are able.

> Pray continually, that ye may not be tempted above that which ye can bear.

I read the verses over and over. I read the ones before, and the ones after, and then reread them all.

Then it struck me. I jumped up from my seat and ran back to my teacher's office.

"I found it!" I exclaimed. "The answer is in the verse itself—look!"

He opened his scriptures to the verses, and I read,

> God is faithful, who will not suffer you to be tempted above that ye are able; but will with the temptation also make a way to escape, that ye may be able to bear it.

I looked up and said, "It doesn't say the devil can't tempt beyond our ability to resist but that the Lord will provide a way for us to escape from such temptations so that we can bear them. And what's the key to escape?" I asked.

I flipped to and read the scripture in Alma:

> But that ye would humble yourselves before the Lord, and call on his holy name, and watch and pray continually, that ye may not be tempted above that which ye can bear.

"The key to escaping temptation is prayer! If we humble ourselves and call on the Lord, that's

SCRIPTURE STUDY *Made Awesome*

the way the Lord has provided for us to escape temptation."

My teacher looked at both verses. "You're right. I can't believe I didn't see that!"

We talked a few more minutes about the supposed contradiction and the wonderful testimony found in the verses about prayer being stronger than the power of Satan. I was reminded of the scripture in the Doctrine and Covenants that says,

> Pray always, that you may come off conqueror; yea, that you may conquer Satan, and that you may escape the hands of the servants of Satan that do uphold his work. (D&C 10:5)

In the apparent contradiction was a beautiful doctrine of the power that comes from always calling on the Lord.

CHAPTER 10

Q & A Methods

Start your study with a question in mind. It can be simple, profound, or even silly, as long as it leads to serious study. Use the Topical Guide, Internet scriptures, or whatever tools you need to find verses that provide an answer to your question. You might even want to make a collection of questions and answers, or add an FAQ (frequently asked questions) section to your notebook.

While serving my mission in South Africa, I became curious about the origins of Africa itself. Who were the first inhabitants there? When did they arrive? How were they different than the native cultures today?

Science has their own ideas about this, many of which are not consistent with modern revelation, so I dedicated several days of my scripture study to find the answer to the question, "Who were the original Africans?"

The result was a fascinating study that took me through all the standard works, especially the Pearl of Great Price and Old Testament. I learned about the flood, the descendents of Ham, the original discovery of Egypt (which, interestingly, was under water when people first found it), and the physical separation of the continents. I'd started the study thinking I wouldn't find much but went away with some cool information and answers to my questions. I even ended up with a bunch more questions, which led to further Q&A studies.

A & Q

Read the scriptures with the idea of finding questions that are answered by the verses. For example, when you get to the verse, "And if it so be that they rebel against me, they shall be a scourge unto thy seed, to stir them up in the ways of remembrance" (1 Nephi 2:24), the question could be, "What happens when we rebel against God?" and the answer, as found in the verse, is

SCRIPTURE STUDY *Made Awesome*

that we become a scourge to generations after us. Another question might be, "Why do some people scourge (persecute) the faithful members of the Church?" or "What purpose can persecution serve for us?"

The scriptures are a book of answers, and it is often a challenge to find the questions. Seeking them out leads to a fascinating study!

WHAT, WHEN, WHERE, WHY, WHO, AND HOW?

After reading a verse, ask yourself, "What is this verse talking about?" Then study to find the answer. Ask the question, "When did this happen?" or "When will this happen?" and then study to find out.

After asking these questions, see if you can figure out why the verse was written and who it was talking about. Do this for each verse you read.

LOVE NOTE Q&A

Pray and ask Heavenly Father a question—any kind of question. Then open your scriptures to a random spot for the answer. Is the answer there? If it doesn't seem to be, dig deeper. Do the verses before and after that verse help? If they don't seem to, try again. Try rephrasing your question in case that makes it easier to find the answer. This might not always answer your questions, but maybe it will offer some insights that you wouldn't have considered otherwise.

SOCIAL NETWORK QUESTION

Come up with a question from a verse of scripture, such as, "What do you suppose Moses thought of when he first reached the Red Sea?" or "What do you suppose Peter did after his denial?" Then post it on your favorite social network. When people respond, look up their ideas in the scriptures to see how plausible they are.

FIND ACTUAL SCRIPTURAL QUESTIONS

Find questions that are actually asked in the scriptures and locate their answers there. For example, consider the verse that says, "What think ye of Christ?" Find a verse that accurately answers this question in a way that matches how you really feel.

The following verses are other scriptural questions that you might consider.

> Have ye experienced this mighty change in
> your hearts? (Alma 5:14)
> Men and brethren, what shall we do?
> (Acts 2:37)
> Whom shall I send? (2 Nephi 16:8)
> Will ye also go away? (John 6:67)

Use one marking method to highlight the question and another for the answer. Then link or cross-reference them.

PLAY THE "WHY?" GAME

Start with a why question of ANY kind. ("Why are clouds white?" or "Why can't cars go faster than two hundred miles per hour?") Then research the answer. Obviously, for non-religious questions, you might have to start with Google. Then ask why that's the answer.

For the clouds question, you'll probably first need to learn something about dust/moisture particles (I'm no meteorologist . . . I'm just supposing), and then ask, "Why do clouds look white?" and find the answer. Then ask why that's the answer.

The deeper you get, the closer you will get to

the scriptural questions, such as, "Why is matter eternal?" and "Why is there no end to space?" or "Why does God love us so much?"

Once you get to these kinds of questions, research the scriptural answers. Then ask why they are the answers, and continue your study.

CHAPTER 11

Deep Study Method

> Do you read the Scriptures, my brethren and sisters, as though you were writing them a thousand, two thousand, or five thousand years ago? Do you read them as though you stood in the place of the men who wrote them? If you do not feel thus, it is your privilege to do so, that you may be as familiar with the spirit and meaning of the written word of God as you are with your daily walk and conversation, or as you are with your workmen or with your households.[1]

Never in the history of the world has there been greater tools to study the gospel of Jesus Christ than what we have today, and the number of these tools will continue to increase.

The edition of the scriptures we use today was organized under the direction of the first presidency in the early 1980s, with the footnotes, Topical Guide, and various other study helps. Of this new set of scriptures, Elder Boyd K. Packer said,

> With the passing of years, these scriptures will produce successive generations of faithful Christians who know the Lord Jesus Christ and are disposed to obey His will.
>
> The older generation has been raised without them, but there is another generation growing up.[2]

Elder David A. Bednar spoke of President Packer's words in general conference and said that the generation Elder Packer was referring to was all of us. That means you.

Elder Packer prophesied that,

> The revelations will be opened to them as to no other in the history of the world. Into their hands now are placed the sticks of Joseph and of Judah. They will develop a gospel scholarship beyond that which their forebears could achieve. They will have the testimony that Jesus is the Christ and be competent to proclaim Him and to defend Him.[3]

That day is here. We're living in a time when

there are more resources to learn, master, and proclaim the gospel than ever before. You can develop a gospel scholarship that exceeds anything earlier members of the Church could achieve. What a great time to be alive!

Let's talk about some ideas of how you can use your study time to deepen your understanding of the gospel and its history and strengthen your personal testimony.

STUDY THE PARABLES IN DETAIL

I love the symbolism and the use of comparisons in the scriptures. One interesting activity is to read a parable (an allegory or a simple comparison) and dig deeper. Get out a dictionary and an encyclopedia and look up Wikipedia on the Internet. (Be sure to check your sources!) Use them to learn more about the subject of the comparison, and search for more ways the comparison applies. Obviously there will many that do not apply, but you can ignore them. You want to find the ones that work. Then search the scriptures for other uses of the same comparison.

I'm sure you heard in Sunday School how the disciples of Jesus are the "salt of the earth."

Perhaps you've heard someone say that salt was used in the Mosaic law for sacrificial offerings, or that salt's savor can only be corrupted by mixing it with another substance. Someone did the research. Now it's your turn. Pick a parable or symbol and start digging!

SEARCH, PONDER, AND PRAY CYCLE

This is an idea I got while at a meeting with Elder Richard G. Scott. He was talking about pondering the scriptures, and he said that as he reads, he stops and ponders individual phrases and prays about them. Then he continues to read. Then he stops, ponders, and prays about the next thing. He later mentioned this method in general conference:

> When I am faced with a very difficult matter, this is how I try to understand what to do. I fast. I pray to find and understand scriptures that will be helpful. That process is cyclical. I start reading a passage of scripture; I ponder what the verse means and pray for inspiration. I then ponder and pray to know if I have captured all the Lord wants me to do. Often more impressions come with increased understanding of doctrine. I have found that pattern to be a good way to learn from the scriptures.[4]

SCRIPTURE STUDY *Made Awesome*

We've all heard about searching, pondering, and praying over the scriptures, but have you ever tried doing it as a cycle, or, in other words, numerous times in a single verse? It's an experience worth having. Begin your study with prayer (as I'm hoping you always do) and start reading. The moment you encounter a concept or a meaningful word, or have a thought on the subject you're reading, stop and think about it. Think deeply about it. Search your mind to see where you lack in understanding or attributes on the topic, and reread the word/phrase. Then pray about it. Ask God to help you better understand it. Then think more on it, and read it again.

As you find new insight coming on, read the next word/phrase and then stop and think about that one. Read it many times. Try to form your mind around the concept. Why did the Lord put this here? What is He trying to tell you? Pray about it and think more on it. Listen for the Spirit and try to remember some experiences you've had or meaningful lessons you've learned on the subject. As you begin to learn, pray for confirmation that what you're learning is correct. Think on what you feel and learn.

Continue this cycle for whatever time you have for study. This is one of the most powerful scripture study methods I've encountered. It takes great energy and concentration, but it's worth the effort! And it's one you can use for as many study sessions as you want.

FOOTNOTE STUDY

Start at the beginning of a book, such as the Book of Mormon, and read each verse, stopping at the footnotes and reading every cross reference. If it says TG and the subject interests you, go to the Topical Guide and read at least some of the verses under that topic.

FOOTNOTE THE SCRIPTURES

Pretend the Church leaders called and told you, "We've decided to completely redo the footnotes in the scriptures, and we'd like you to help."

Create new footnotes. You can use the footnotes already there to help you in deciding on new footnotes if you want to, but don't automatically include them. Don't forget to include cross-referenced scriptures, Topical Guide references (or create your own topical guide, as we will discuss in a moment), IEs (in explanation), and alternate translations, such as Greek, Hebrew, and Reformed Egyptian. (Good luck with that one!)

CREATE YOUR OWN TOPICAL GUIDE

Create a new topical guide. You can either start with a subject and find every scripture you can locate on it, or you can start at the beginning of a book and pull scriptures by topic. As an example, if you're reading 1 Nephi 1:1, you can put this verse in a number of topics:

> I, NEPHI, having been born of goodly parents, therefore I was taught somewhat in all the learning of my father; and having seen many afflictions in the course of my days, nevertheless, having been highly favored of the Lord in all my days; yea, having had a great knowledge of the goodness and the mysteries of God, therefore I make a record of my proceedings in my days. (1 Nephi 1:1)

That verse alone can be put under the topics Nephi, Lehi, Parenthood, Teaching, Learn,

Fatherhood, Afflictions, Trials, Suffering, God's Favor, Goodness, Mysteries, Mysteries of God (or you can list it as God, Mysteries of—if you prefer), Record Keeping, Scriptures, Journal Keeping, and Knowledge of God. And don't limit yourself to the subjects you might find in the existing topical guide. Come up with your own subjects, especially those that might help you in your personal or family life. Putting this verse under all those subjects will build your topical guide fast, and by the time you've finished the first chapter, you'll have quite a collection. Just think how much you'll have when you've gone through the entire Book of Mormon!

Use a notebook, an address book, or a computer (my personal recommendation) to keep your homemade topical guide. If this method works well for you, go on to the other standard works. You might find that *your* topical guide is more useful to you than the regular topical guide.

CHRONOLOGICAL NEW TESTAMENT STUDY

In the Bible Dictionary under "Gospels, Harmony of," there's a form that shows the chronology of events recorded in the four gospels. Using the chart as a guide, study the entire New Testament chronologically. Don't forget to check the footnotes for JSTs and alternate translations.

LOOK FOR THE SMALLER DETAILS

As you read, look for the unnoticed details that you don't usually see. For example, in this verse:

> And there were no envyings, nor strifes, nor tumults, nor whoredoms, nor lyings, nor murders, nor any manner of lasciviousness; and surely there could not be a happier people among all the people who had been created by the hand of God. (4 Nephi 1:16)

What is meant by "tumults?"

Why is the word "surely" there?

Why is it written "the hand of God" instead of just "God?"

Keep a running list of these questions in your study notebook, and as you either study and find the answers, or bump into them later, write them in your scripture notebook or journal.

LOOK FOR KNOW, FEEL, DO

When reading the scriptures, look for verses that represent these three actions: 1) learning something (know), 2) feeling the confirming witness of its truth or reacting emotionally to the teaching (feel), and 3) acting on the knowledge you have gained (do). As you read each verse, identify which is being represented. Decide on a marking for each (such as a bracket around the verse for "know," a circle for "feel," and a square for "do"—or perhaps a different color for each). Try to mark your scriptures throughout with knows, feels, and dos. Keep in mind that many verses will overlap, and some will have all three represented in a single verse.

THE MCCONKIE TEST

Elder Bruce R. McConkie suggested this method:

> May I be so bold as to propose a test and issue a challenge . . .
>
> Let every person make a list of from one hundred to two hundred doctrinal subjects, making a conscious effort to cover the whole field of gospel knowledge . . .

Then write each subject on a blank piece of paper. Divide the paper into two columns. At the top of one, write "Book of Mormon," and at the top of the other, "Bible."

Then start with the first verse and phrase of the Book of Mormon, and continuing verse by verse and thought by thought, put the substance of each verse under its proper heading. Find the same doctrine in the Old and New Testaments, and place it in the parallel columns.[5]

LOOK FOR PROMISES, WARNINGS, DOCTRINES, AND COMMANDMENTS

When the Lord speaks in scripture, he nearly always gives a promise, a warning, a doctrine, or a commandment. Search for the these four messages in each verse you read, and use a four-color pen (or choose four different techniques from chapter 6, pages 36–40) and mark them. This works especially well in the Doctrine and Covenants where nearly the entire book is direct revelation from Jesus Christ. The following is an example from the Book of Mormon:

> 33 Therefore, keep these sayings which I have commanded you that ye come not under condemnation; for wo unto him whom the Father condemneth.
>
> 34 And I give you these commandments because of the disputations which have been among you. And blessed are ye if ye have no disputations among you.
>
> 35 And now I go unto the Father, because it is expedient that I should go unto the Father for your sakes. (3 Nephi 18:33–35)

Can you see any promises, warnings, doctrines, or commandments in these verses?

Marking verses in this way can be a fun activity to help you get more from your scripture reading.

CREATE A "TEACHINGS OF" COLLECTION

Have you ever heard of the book *Scriptural Teachings of Joseph Smith*? It's a collection of the Prophet's teachings, organized by topic. Similar books have been written with the topical teachings of each of the modern-day prophets.

Create your own "book" (more likely pamphlet, but you get the idea) of the teachings of your favorite scriptural prophet, and organize them alphabetically by topic. Say, for example, your choice is Ammon, who taught King Lamoni. What did Ammon teach about the Atonement? Baptism? Charity? Discipline? Eternal Life? Faith? God? Honesty? See what I mean? You can find lessons on each of these topics just from Ammon's experiences, and the topics would cover nearly the entire alphabet. You don't have to limit it just to what they said, either. You can also find lessons in how they lived and what they did.

THE OLD HEBREW PROVERB

You've probably heard people say, "Have you ever heard the old Chinese Proverb that says . . . ?" then they recite some cool quote that is applicable to many situations.

If you've never taken a serious look at the book of Proverbs in the Bible, read it. It's essentially a collection of old Hebrew proverbs—short one- or two-sentence quotes that have wide application.

If you want to make more than a few study sessions out of it, read the footnote cross references as you go along. You might even want to try memorizing a few of your favorites.

SCRIPTURAL PEOPLE LIST

Create an alphabetical list of people in the scriptures. Use either copied and pasted scriptures, or at least copied references to the relevant verses. Write a three- or four-sentence bio of each. (If there's that much info in the scriptures about that person.)

Start at the beginning of each book. As you come across people, add them to the list, along with the reference of where you found them. People like Nephi will have substantial references, but just keep adding them alphabetically as you go. You never know when this list will come in handy!

SCRIPTURAL PLACES LIST

Similar to the Scriptural People List, create an alphabetical list of scriptural places. Do it the same way you did the people list. If you can find enough information, write three or four sentences of detail about each place.

Start at the beginning of each book. As you come across places, add them to the list, along with the reference of where you found them. Places like Jerusalem will have substantial references, but just keep adding them alphabetically as you go. This list may also come in handy some day!

FIND THE LORD'S TENDER MERCIES

A number of years ago, Elder David A. Bednar gave a powerful conference talk about the Lord's tender mercies. As he defines them, "The Lord's tender mercies are the very personal and individualized blessings, strength, protection, assurances, guidance, loving-kindnesses, consolation, support, and spiritual gifts which we receive from, because of, and through the Lord Jesus Christ."[6]

Basically, the tender mercies of the Lord are those simple acts of kindness that He does for us to help or show us He loves us.

Look for examples of the Lord's tender mercies as you read the scriptures. They might seem hard to find at first, but the more you search, the more you will find, until you are marking almost every verse, sometimes multiple times.

CREATE A SCRIPTURAL CHRONOLOGY

As you probably know, many of the scriptures are not given in the order they happened.

They are organized by size or as a reference to something in the past or in the future.

With as much detail as you can, create a chronology of the events in the scriptures. Use whatever resources you need to verify the accuracy of the chronology. For a while you'll probably be mixing the Old Testament and Pearl of Great Price. Soon the book of Ether will come in, and if you are keeping it chronological right down to each verse, you'll have an interesting collection that will offer some powerful insights into how the Lord's hand is in His creations and in the lives of His children.

Henry B. Eyring said,

> You can study the word of God, not for yourself alone but to be an emissary of the Lord Jesus Christ to all the world. When you increase your power to teach the gospel, you are qualifying to help Heavenly Father in gathering His children. As you do that, another blessing will come. Should the need ever come in family life in this world, or in the world to come, to draw back lost sheep, you will have received more power than you may now recognize.[7]

USE THE INSTITUTE MANUALS AND OTHER STUDY GUIDES

The Church publishes a number of great scripture study guides. My personal favorite is the institute student manuals, intended as supplements to institute classes. They have a manual for each of the modern standard works, and three for the Bible. Get copies from the distribution center, or access them for free online at http://institute.lds.org/courses/. Follow along in the manual and do any assignments you come across. You will find amazing information, history, and insight in these books.

STUDY THE CONTEXT

Learning the political, geographic, and historical context of the scriptures and the background of the prophets who wrote them can offer a lot of insight. Stop reading from time to time to find out who said what, where they were when they said it, and what was going on around them when they said it. Also, see if you can find out *why* it was said. Was it spoken to an audience, written for posterity, or given as personal revelation to someone? Find as much context around the verse as possible.

RECITE THE SCRIPTURES BY MEMORY

This is good to try if you want to get better at memorizing verses, or if you forget to take your scriptures with you somewhere. With no scriptures in hand, try to recite the Book of Mormon from memory. Start with "I Nephi" and see how far you get. When you get stuck, find the next place you *can* remember and continue—but make note of the spot you got stuck. See how much you remember.

If 1 Nephi is tough, pick some other place in the scriptures and try reciting the entire chapter or section. When you're done, go back to see what you missed. Study those areas. Develop a strong understanding of them. You might find that studying them will do more to help you recall the missed areas than rote memorization.

LIST TEN SCRIPTURES BY VALUE

Not all scriptures have the same value. Find a random verse in your computerized scriptures and copy the verse into a text document (or manually find and write them on a paper). Repeat this procedure ten times so that you have ten random scriptures. Then put them in order of importance, the top being the most important—or highest message—and on down.

SCRIPTURAL THANKAMONY

Pray and tell your Heavenly Father how grateful you are for your blessings—one by one. Stop every couple of minutes and look up scriptures about the things you are grateful for. See if you can learn more about God's plan concerning your blessings.

WRITE YOUR OWN SCRIPTURAL COMMENTARY

Create your own scripture commentary. Use a computer with a word processing program and write the scripture. Then follow it up with cross references, quotes, thoughts, feelings, ideas, insights, and anything else that might make for interesting study. Look up talks and firesides on the subject, and paste the most relevant parts into your commentary.

WRITE YOUR OWN VERSION OF THE SCRIPTURES

You've probably seen the New International version of the Bible, as well as a dozen other versions. In the Church we are encouraged to focus on the King James version, with the footnotes as guides. But for your own personal use and study, there's no reason you can't create your own version of the scriptures. I once heard that Bruce R. McConkie did this and then threw them away when he was done because the learning came in the creation of them and not in later study. Do this yourself. Create your own version of the Book of Mormon or Bible—in your own words. (You don't have to throw them away later if you don't want to.)

MENTALLY SWITCH ROLES

Take different scripture characters and mentally switch their roles. What if Nephi had been in Ammon's place? How would he have done things differently? Or you can even switch people from different sides. What if Moroni somehow was designated as leader of the Lamanites in place of Ammonihah? How would things have turned out differently?

SCRIPTURE STUDY *Made Awesome*

Don't stop at, "Oh, then the war would have ended." Consider *how* the war would have ended. What can you learn about Moroni's personality that might give a clue about the ultimate outcome of the situation?

Try it with characters from different books or eras. What would Ammon have been like in Elijah's place? Or Eve in Emma's place? Write your thoughts in your journal or scripture notebook.

WRITE YOUR OWN SCRIPTURES

Imagine you were commissioned by Nephi to continue the scriptures, as he did with his younger brother. Write your scriptures in your journal or scripture notebook, and remember that the assignment from Nephi was to focus on things spiritual. You can quote other verses of scripture, but make sure you comment on them as Nephi did. Write your own spiritual experiences, and try to write them in scriptural language.

TRANSLATE A BOOK OF SCRIPTURE

If you know another language, translate the scriptures into that language. Translating often gives insights into verses that can be otherwise hard to find. Another way to do this is to take a book of scripture in your second language, find a chapter you aren't completely familiar with, and translate it into English. When you're done, compare it with the English version to see how you did.

If you want, you can try to do it in just a few months like Joseph Smith did. That might provide some insights into his experience!

FIND CHIASMUS

Chiasmus is a Hebrew writing style in which ideas are written in one order and then mirrored or written in the reverse order. A chiasmus can also be the repetition of opposites in an inverted order. An example of the first definition might be, "The first shall be last, and the last shall be first" (see Matthew 19:30). This is a mirrored chiasmus. The second definition might be comparable to "Whosoever shall lose his life for my sake, shall find it" (see JST, Matthew 16:28). This example inverts opposites. Chiasmus is such an important part of Hebrew writing that the scriptures are *filled* with it. Go through the scriptures and mark a chiasmus wherever you can find it.

SCRIPTURE STUDY *Made Awesome*

In addition to verses that contain chiasmi, you can sometimes find entire chapters or books that are written in this way. Here's a simple, made-up chiasmus so you can clearly understand the concept.

1. We are children of God
    2. We've been sent to earth
        3. We have families here
            4. We sin and make mistakes
                5. Jesus Christ saves us from sin by our repentance
                6. We are forgiven through the Savior's Atonement
            7. We overcome our mistakes
        8. We teach our children righteousness
    9. We die and leave the earth
10. We return to God

If you line up the ideas, you can see that 1 and 10 both relate to us being the children of God, 2 and 9 are opposites (we come to earth and we die), and 3 and 8 both talk about families.

Analyze the scriptures to find as many chiasmi as you can. This is a powerful concept, because in Hebrew, the main idea is usually found within the verses, words, or chapters in the middle of the chiasmus. Or, in other words, numbers 5 and 6 of our example are the central point of the entire message. Knowing this and searching for a chiasmus can help identify what the prophets were trying to emphasize.

Though not necessarily a chiasmus, it's interesting to note that Hebrews tend to give emphasis in the opposite order that we do. For example, as a twenty-first century American, if I were to talk about progressing toward flight, I might say I'd learn to walk, then run, then fly. I'd place emphasis by saving the important thing for last. But Hebrews often prefer to put the emphasis first. So, instead of using my order, they would start with the end. "They shall mount up with wings as eagles; they shall run, and not be weary; and they shall walk, and not faint" (see Isaiah 40:31).

This sounds backward to us, but it's the way a Hebrew would write it to emphasize the flight. Look for reverse progression like this in the scriptures. It's fairly common.

REREAD THE SAME CHAPTER TEN TIMES

Pick a chapter to study and read it ten times. Seek to glean as much as possible from each

SCRIPTURE STUDY *Made Awesome*

reading. You might be surprised at how much you can get out of your ninth and tenth readings. You might want to note your observations in your notebook. Try linking your insights to which number of reading you're on.

LOOK FOR FACTS, PRINCIPLES, AND DOCTRINES

The scriptures are full of teachings, and most can be divided into facts, principles, or doctrines. Pick a marking method for each and label your scriptures based on the subject matter.

EARN YOUR YW MEDALLION OR DUTY TO GOD AWARD

No matter your age, meet the requirements for getting your Young Women Medallion or your Duty to God Award. They involve a lot of scripture study and journal writing, so be thorough in your assignments.

WORD-BY-WORD DEFINITION STUDY

We've all heard talks in church where the speaker uses the dictionary to define the word pertaining to his or her topic. Do this as you study, but instead of looking up just one word, look up every possible word in the verse. More specifically, look up every noun, verb, and adjective. They are most likely the ones that give the verse its meaning.

When you come across pronouns, such as he, she, or it, find the antecedent. Who is the "he" referring to? What is "it?"

You might even want to find an 1830's dictionary since Joseph Smith was transcribing in nineteenth century English, which is slightly different than twenty-first century English.

Don't forget to look up groups of words. Many word groupings have meanings unique to that set of words, such as idioms and cultural clichés.

The Topical Guide and Bible Dictionary might help with many of the scriptural terms, and if you cross-reference the word you are studying with other verses that share that word, you might be able to find more insight into the meaning of the word or phrase.

FIND THE SCRIPTURAL DEFINITION

Finding scriptural definitions is different than finding dictionary definitions. For example, the scriptures often use the word *mystery* and encourage us to seek out the mysteries. But our modern definition, even in LDS culture, gives the impression that a mystery is something unknown and strange—possibly even forbidden. The scriptures never discourage us from seeking out the mysteries of God, even though church leaders *do* often discourage it. This is not because they contradict one another. It's simply because the scriptures use a different definition for the word *mystery* than we do in our culture. One definition is not wrong—just different.

As you read the scriptures, don't assume that you know what a word means. As an example, dig to find out what *Lord* means when He uses it, or what the prophets meant when they wrote it. When you discover these definitions, write them in your scriptures and cross-reference other major references to your chosen word so whenever you come across it, you can understand it with its intended meaning.

Looking for the scriptural definition of words can be a fun way to engage with the scriptures. Start on the first verse of a chapter and see how many words you can find that have unique scriptural definitions.

Incidentally, when the scriptures talk about mysteries, they seem to be referring simply to knowledge obtained by the power of the Holy Ghost.

If you want a head start, try researching the scriptural definitions of these words or terms:

TODAY
THE NAME OF CHRIST
WEAKNESS
GRACE
BABYLON
ZION
HOPE
PROPHECY
LIGHT
DEATH

WHAT IS DIFFERENT?

Find two verses that appear identical in two different books of scripture and write or copy and paste them side by side in your study journal or on a piece of paper. Then look especially close. Is there *any* difference? If not, find another identical verse. When you find two nearly identical verses that only have a subtle, seemingly insignificant difference, study them carefully. What does the subtle difference actually do to the verses? What is the function of the "to" instead of "of," or perhaps the "will" instead of "have"? How does the tiny difference change the verse and meaning?

WRITE A CHILDREN'S VERSION OF THE SCRIPTURES

Rewrite the scriptures in such a way that children can easily understand them. Don't shorten or summarize them. Just reword individual verses for young minds.

If you're a parent, this could be an especially useful method. Recently, as Jenni was reading the story of Esther to our six-year-old daughter, our daughter said, "Why was the king mad at the other queen?"

Jenni looked it up, and after a few minutes, she finally said, "She didn't come to dinner."

"Oh."

Later, Jenni and I talked about how it would have been nice for her to have read through the verses beforehand. That way she would have been prepared to explain what was going on. This simple incident made us want to read some of the less familiar aspects of the scripture stories we hear so often.

Elder Richard G. Scott said,

> Because scriptures are generated from inspired communication through the Holy Ghost, they are pure truth. We need not be concerned about the validity of concepts contained in the standard works since the Holy Ghost has been the instrument which has motivated and inspired those individuals who have recorded the scriptures.[8]

VERSE BY VERSE SUMMARY

Start at the beginning of a book of scripture and write in a notebook or document a three- to ten-word summary of each verse. I tried this a number of years ago, and I got though half the Book of Mormon this way. It was interesting trying to decide what words would best describe the verse. It also helped me remember what happened in individual chapters of scripture.

CONNECTIONS, PATTERNS, AND THEMES

Elder David A. Bednar provided this method when he said,

> I now want to review with you three basic ways or methods of obtaining living water from the scriptural reservoir: (1) *reading* the scriptures from beginning to end, (2) *studying* the scriptures by topic, and (3) *searching* the scriptures for connections, patterns, and themes. Each of these approaches can help satisfy our spiritual thirst if we invite the companionship and assistance of the Holy Ghost as we read, study, and search.[9]

STUDY THE BAD GUYS

Sometimes we focus so much on what the good guys are doing that we forget to notice the lessons taught by the bad examples of the bad guys. Study the bad guys in the scriptures and notice the words and sins that made them what they became.

NOTES

1. Brigham Young, *Discourses of Brigham Young* (Salt Lake City: Deseret Book, 1954), 128.

2. Boyd K. Packer, in Conference Report, October 1982, 75; or *Ensign*, November 1982, 53.

3. Boyd K. Packer, as quoted in David A. Bednar's "A Reservoir of Living Water," BYU Speeches, February 4, 2007. (See http://speeches.byu.edu/?act=viewitem&id=1686; accessed March 20, 2013.)

4. Richard G. Scott, "How to Obtain Revelation and Inspiration for Your Personal Life," *Ensign*, May 2012, 45–47.

5. Bruce R. McConkie, "What Think Ye of the Book of Mormon?" *Ensign*, November 1983, 72.

6. David A. Bednar, "The Tender Mercies of the Lord," *Ensign*, April 2005, 99.

7. Henry B. Eyring, "Faith and the Oath and Covenant of the Priesthood," *Ensign*, May 2008, 61–64.

8. Richard G. Scott, "The Power of Scripture," *Ensign*, November 2011, 6.

9. Bednar, "A Reservoir of Living Water."

CHAPTER 12

Creative Methods

READ A MOVIE

Read slowly and try to visualize everything that's happening in the scriptures, in even more detail than what is given. Imagine you're watching a movie, and try to picture everything, including the expressions, gestures, emotions, clothing, and landscape. When you read, "I said unto my father, I will go and do the things which the Lord hath commanded" (1 Nephi 3:7), try to see Nephi's face. If it helps, imagine an actor playing the part of Nephi and another for Lehi. Picture Lehi's concerned expression and Nephi's determined look. What are Nephi's hands doing? Is he holding something? Is he gripping his father's arm? Play the entire thing out in your mind as you slowly read so you can even hear the tone of the narrator's voice.

It might help to have appropriate soundtrack music playing in the background. Playing *Pirates of the Caribbean* music while reading about a war can really be fun.

Don't hold back on this. You might walk away from scripture study feeling as if you were really there. This can be mentally exhausting. Let it be. You'll gain insights that you might not have gotten any other way.

QUICKLY DRAW WHAT'S HAPPENING

Listen to the scriptures and draw everything that's going on. Use simple pictures like stick figures, and try to portray the events. As events change, you can either draw them in separate frames like a comic book, or try to reflect the events in a larger single picture. If Nephi is building a boat, draw the tools, the mountain, and even the billows. If you're feeling artsy, you could even use symbols, shapes, or interesting images for representations—such as a bow-like shape to represent Nephi and a tree to represent Lehi. Then symbolically represent the events

SCRIPTURE STUDY *Made Awesome*

taking place with the images surrounding the subjects.

SLOWLY DRAW WHAT'S HAPPENING

If you are an artist, listen to a chapter or group of chapters surrounding an event that you'd like to draw or paint. Choose the scene carefully and listen to the chapter as you draw. When you get to the end of the chapter or group of chapters, repeat them. Listen to the verses dozens of times as you draw. Something late in the chapter might feed the mood or details of the picture. You don't have to capture all the details or even represent all that takes place. As you listen to the chapter, just listen for subtle details that might influence how you draw.

MONOLOGUE READING

If you're remotely interested in acting, this one can really be a lot of fun and bring the scriptures to life. Find a place where you can speak freely without being heard, and bring your scriptures. Then read out loud, using the most interesting and dramatically appropriate tone of voice possible. For example, if you're reading a war chapter, read quick, loud, and intensely as if you're commentating as the war is actually taking place. Then, if you're reading the words of a prophet, speak in the gentle, firm, or shouting voice that seems most fitting. You can even use accents and unique voices for individual speakers. Pretend you're a master of Shakespearean monologue, reciting the well-versed words of a play.

You might find yourself having so much fun that you won't want to stop!

MAP THE WARS AND TRAVELS

As you read a part of the scriptures that deal with either war or travel, use your notebook or computer to create a map of the scene/place you're reading about. If there is a chase going on, draw arrows going around the mountain or through the river depending on where the action takes place in the verses. If you prefer, use audio verses so you can map it as you listen. If you don't feel comfortable inventing a fresh map, get a printout or a pdf of either the Bible maps or the map in the Book of Mormon institute manual that is based on internal evidences.

Jenni likes to take distances such as "one day's journey" and designate a certain length for them. For instance, one inch equals one day's journey. This helps her map the distances between locations.

TAKE A MAP TOUR

Get out one of the Bible maps and begin at one of the edges. Walk your finger from that edge, and each time you come across a new city, use the Topical Guide and Bible Dictionary to look up what happened in that city in the scriptures.

You might even want to pop open Google Earth or Google Maps satellite and street view to see what the city looks like now.

MAKE A LABELED DIAGRAM OF THE SCRIPTURES

Remember those labeled diagrams we were given in school that had lines leading to descriptions? Try making a labeled diagram for the verse of scripture you are studying. You could link to a word or phrase and label it, "The Lord's instruction to missionaries," or "The reason agency is so important." Come up with labels for as many things in the verse that you can.

Chas HATHAWAY

REFORMAT INTO POETIC STYLE

Take a verse of scripture and reformat the structure into a style that makes it look like poetry. Do as many verses as necessary to make it a complete "poem." For example:

HE DID HEAL THEM
And it came to pass
That when he had thus spoken,
All the multitude,
With one accord,
Did go forth with their sick
        And their afflicted,
        And their lame,
        And with their blind,
        And with their dumb,
And with all them that were afflicted
In any manner;
And he did heal them
Every one
As they were brought forth
Unto him.
        (3 Nephi 17:9)

REWRITE THE VERSES INTO RHYMING POETRY

Turn the verse into a rhyme, keeping the meaning as close to the original as possible.

Record the verses in a book or pamphlet of scriptural poems. It might help to have a thesaurus and/or rhyming dictionary handy. As an example:

> **BROUGHT FORTH TO HIM**
> And it came to pass that when he was done,
> all the multitude, every one,
> Inviting their sick, and to him they came
> Their sick, and afflicted, their blind and
>   their lame
> Restoring their bodies, both heartache and limb
> Everyone as they were brought forth to him.
>
> (See 3 Nephi 17:9.)

STUDY WHILE DOING OTHER THINGS

Listen to the scriptures while you do other things. Some people can concentrate better if their hands and bodies are busy. Listen to the scriptures when you draw or paint, or when you do the dishes, mow the lawn, or carry out other chores. Take an MP3 player or mobile phone on a walk or a jog. Car rides can be a great way to clear the mind, so try listening to the scriptures while you drive. You can also listen to conference talks, BYU speeches, CES firesides, or lesson manuals (even those are available in audio). If your job allows earbuds, listen at work. You'll be surprised how many chapters you can read with three or four hours of listening.

Listening at work was a pivotal event in my own spiritual journey. I had a part-time job all through high school, two hours every weeknight. I dreaded going to work—until one night I brought a cassette Walkman (yeah, I'm that old) to work and listened to the Doctrine and Covenants cassettes I'd been given for Christmas the previous year.

From then on I'd go to work, pop in a tape, and about fifteen sections later, I'd go home. It didn't take long to get through the Doctrine and Covenants. So, with my paycheck, I bought the Book of Mormon on cassette and whizzed through it a couple of times. I collected all of the standard works on cassette and eventually the most recent conference talks. I even started renting talks on tape from the library.

Before long I found that I knew almost all the answers in seminary and was constantly raising my hand in Sunday School. I was fully participating in gospel discussions. It was exhilarating!

I remember waking up and not being able to go back to sleep one night when I was a teenager. I decided to listen to the scriptures, so I popped one of the Book of Mormon cassettes into a small boom box next to my bed and began to listen. It was winter, and the heater was starting up again, so I jumped out of bed, brought my blanket to the vent, and sat, listening to the word of God.

I remember my cozy blanket heating up around me, and the warm sensation of the Spirit as I listened to the inspired messages of the Book of Mormon. I don't know how long I sat there, listening and feeling, but that experience changed me.

I came to love the scriptures and the words of the prophets so much that every time I did chores or worked in the yard, I'd listen to my cassettes. I'd listen to talks, scriptures, or other uplifting media every chance I got.

Come to think of it, I still do.

We have so many advantages nowadays. The scriptures, conference talks, lesson manuals, and BYU speeches are all free MP3 downloads on the Church's and BYU's websites. A simple MP3 player will hold all of the standard works, as well as all the general conference talks since 1971.

SHARE VERSES ON SOCIAL MEDIA OR EMAIL

If you use the Internet and are connected to any social networks, read the scriptures and look for something to share with someone online. Perhaps you have a friend whose family member is struggling with his or her health. Find a scripture about the power of coming to know God through tribulation and share it with your friend. Then look for another verse to share with someone else.

This can work with other kinds of social networks as well. I was following some religious discussions on a forum awhile back, and someone started a thread on Mormonism. Although the person who started the thread was doing his best to defend our religion, there were a lot of antagonistic contributors to the discussion, and it was becoming unfair toward members of the Church. I got involved, and the discussions continued. Some people addressed the Church fairly, while others did not. The conversation continued for some time.

At one point I got a direct email from one of the people in the conversation. She essentially wanted to know why I believed in the doctrine of the LDS Church. She didn't believe in it, and she couldn't understand why anyone else would. It gave me the opportunity to share my testimony, and even though she never came to believe in it for herself, she was moved by the things I shared. The conversation that went back and forth by email was a testament to me of the power of sharing the gospel online.

Share scriptures and feelings on your own social networks. Some people will disagree with what you say, but don't get defensive. Thank them for their comments and stand by the truth you share.

SHADOW READ

While listening to the scriptures on your MP3 player or mobile device, repeat the words of the reader within a second or two of him saying them. You'd be surprised how challenging it is. Make a goal to read an entire chapter aloud without stopping.

PLAY AN LDS TRIVIA GAME

Play an LDS trivia game, like Jots and Tittles, Seek, Zion, or any other LDS scripture-based trivia game. Find a question to which you don't know the answer—the tougher the question, the better. Without looking at the answer, spend whatever time necessary researching the answer from the scriptures. Don't look at the answer on the back of the card until you are sure you've found the correct answer for yourself.

CREATE AN LDS TRIVIA GAME

As you read the scriptures, gather questions from the verses and create your own LDS trivia game. For example, starting with 1 Nephi 1:1, "Who was the first author in the Book of Mormon?," "What term did Nephi use to describe his parents?," and "What languages did Lehi teach Nephi?"

By the time you've read the scriptures through, you'll have a hefty list of questions that could be used for your own LDS trivia game. You might even want to rank questions by difficulty as you write them. That first question might be a level 2; the second, a level 4; and so on. If you collect the questions on the computer, such as in a document or a spreadsheet, you can even color-code them by level. Then use the trivia questions in family home evening or to test yourself later.

SCRIPTURE COLLAGE

Cut up magazines, newspapers, and junk mail and paste words together in a collage of your favorite scripture. For words you can't find, use individual letters or groups of letters. As you find each word, consider why that word was used. Write your thoughts on your considerations in your scriptural journal. If the writing goes well, take a photo of your collage to put in your journal as a souvenir of the experience.

STUDY HYMNBOOK SCRIPTURES

Open the hymnbook and turn to a favorite hymn. Study the verses listed at the end of the hymn. See if you can find more scriptures that relate to it. Once you have finished working with one, move on to another. There are enough hymns with scriptures to give you weeks of study if you enjoy doing this.

I have a friend who does this, and she writes the name of the hymn by the verse that applies to it so she can refer back to it when she comes across that scripture again.

NAME THAT HYMN

Go to the "Scriptures" section at the back of the hymnbook where the scriptural references are found. Choose a random spot and look up the scripture. Try to guess which hymn belongs with the verses. After you make your guess, look up the hymn number to see if you guessed accurately.

WRITE A HYMN

The Lord has said, "My soul delighteth in the song of the heart; yea, the song of the righteous is a prayer unto me, and it shall be answered with a blessing upon their heads" (D&C 25:12). Study a verse or scriptural topic that especially interests you and write a hymn based on those scriptures. If necessary, look up quotes by general authorities to make sure the doctrine is correct. If it goes well and you like the results, submit it to the music section of the

Church website. Who knows, your study might be in the next hymnbook!

ADD ILLUSTRATIONS TO YOUR SCRIPTURES

Buy the illustrated scripture story books found at the distribution center. Cut out the pictures and paste them into your own standard works. If you're using digital scriptures, screen-capture the images, place them in a simple image editing program, and paste them into your digital scriptures.

MODERNIZE THE PARABLES

Study a favorite parable or allegory from the scriptures. Make sure you understand the symbols used, based on doctrine, culture, and context. Rewrite the parable for modern times. Use symbols that are familiar to us in the twenty-first century, such as cars, computers, Facebook, schools, libraries, or whatever best fits the parable.

SCRIPTURE STUDY SOUNDTRACK

Create a new playlist on Pandora, iTunes, Playlist, Spotify, or your favorite music source that has good background music for reading the scriptures. Create a special compilation for the action chapters (those that include war or destruction), one for the touching, emotional chapters, and one for the trial-based chapters, and so on. Find music to match the mood of the story and play the appropriate compilation as you read. You might get so emotionally involved that you find yourself reading a lot longer than you'd planned.

BUBBLE DIAGRAMS

Remember the diagrams with something in the middle of the page with a bubble around it, and lines connecting that bubble to other bubbles, and more lines connecting those bubbles to more bubbles? Write a verse or portion of a verse in the middle of a page (as small as you can) and put a bubble around it. Then write another verse near the first bubble, put a bubble around it, and connect it with a line to the first bubble. Add more verses and bubble them, connecting them with other bubbled scriptures that have something in common with them. For example, you

SCRIPTURE STUDY *Made Awesome*

might have Nephi's "go and do" verse connected to the stripling warrior's verse about obeying with exactness, and the "go and do" verse also connected to a verse in Alma 37 about why the scriptures are so essential. Then you could connect verses that refer to obeying prophetic guidance to the stripling warrior verse.

CHAPTER 13

Family Scripture Study Methods

TAKE TURNS

The most common method of reading as a family is probably to take turns, with each family member reading one or two verses. Try having the last reader choose the next reader. It might keep potential between-turn sleepers alert.

BOOK OF MORMON GAME

This is one of my favorites. Have someone step to the front of the room with their Book of Mormon and start reading at a random spot. Then everyone else races through their own books to see who can find the spot first. When someone finds it, instead of raising a hand or shouting out where it is, he or she reads along (thus verifying that it is really the right spot). That person is then "it" and gets to go to the front and read from a random spot.

You might want to warn the group ahead of time to choose their "random spot" before beginning to make sure there aren't any dead giveaways in it. If there are, they can choose a different spot. Once they start reading, however, they have to keep reading until someone starts reading along. They should leave out chapter headings and continue on to the next chapter as if there were no chapter break.

This might also provide a good opportunity to teach new readers about the index and Topical Guide. As an example, when the person reads, "did gather his armies together upon the hill Comnor" (Ether 14:28), everyone can rush to the index to look for "Comnor" to help them find the spot.

BOOK OF MORMON RISK

This is a great family home evening activity that could potentially take hours.

Play Risk with normal rules[1]—except every time two players would normally roll the dice

SCRIPTURE STUDY *Made Awesome*

to battle, do this instead: have someone read a random spot in the scriptures (Book of Mormon works best for our family), and the two players each guess the book, chapter, and verse they think it is. (No cheating with their own scriptures!) Whoever guesses closest wins the battle as if they rolled the winning dice. If they're within the same chapter, it counts as two battles won (unless it's countered by the other person *also* being within the same chapter). If someone guesses the verse right on, then it's total elimination, meaning that if they were the attacker, they wiped out all of the defending armies except the one retreating army; and if they're a defender, they wiped out the entire attacking army. This one is a blast. It makes the players want to learn the scriptures better!

You can also use this method as a scripture chase. A single verse is read, and the first of two players to find it in their own scriptures wins the battle.

SCRIPTURE TRIVIA

Come up with a question (or find one in a Book of Mormon or Bible trivia game) that no one in the family knows the answer to, and then work together to find the answer in the scriptures. We've mentioned this method as an individual study method, but it can be a lot of fun to do as a family, because you can discuss things as you find them.

READ THE SCRIPTURES LIKE A MELODRAMA

Read the scriptures out loud to the children. Every time a good guy speaks, or the people in the verse do something good, have everyone cheer. When the bad guy speaks, or the people do something bad, have everyone boo.

USE TOYS FOR YOUNG CHILDREN

For young children, give everyone stuffed animals, dolls, or other toys to do the reading. Give each toy a unique voice and manner. My sister does this with her family and says it works well to keep even the smallest child—and his parents—interested.

RECORD YOURSELVES READING THE BOOK OF MORMON TOGETHER

As you read together as a family, use a mobile phone or a digital recorder to record your family

SCRIPTURE STUDY *Made Awesome*

reading the scriptures together. When you've completed the entire Book of Mormon, give everyone a copy of the MP3s to listen to on their own.

Elder Richard G. Scott did something like this for his family:

> In 1991 I wanted to give a special Christmas gift to my family. In recording the fulfillment of that desire, my personal journal states: "It is 12:38 p.m., Wednesday, December 18, 1991. I've just concluded an audio recording of the Book of Mormon for my family. This has been an experience that has increased my testimony of this divine work and strengthened in me a desire to be more familiar with its pages to distill from these scriptures truths to be used in my service to the Lord. I love this book."[2]

MEMORIZATION GAME

Have the family memorize a number of verses together (perhaps scripture masteries or the Primary themes). Play an ongoing game throughout the day where you shout out a reference, such as "John 3:16!" The first person to fully recite it gets a point or a prize. Give extra points or rewards to everyone if they can recite it together in unison. If you use points, consider adding them up and using them for a reward at your next Family Home Evening.

Jenni told me that when she memorizes a verse of scripture, it's more likely to come into her head at moments when she needs it. She has the words going through her head so much from memorizing them that they easily slip back into her head when they apply to a given situation. This can happen with children, too. Don't get upset if they are singing verses of scripture to ridiculous tunes and reciting them in pointless repetitive games, because they are solidifying those scriptures in their minds and hearts for when they need them later.

SWITCH READERS WITH EVERY WORD

When reading together as a family, switch readers with every word instead of with every verse. The one who stops or breaks the flow gets "buzzed" by the rest of the family. The family scores when they make it through an entire verse without pausing.

PRIMARY VERSES

If your children are in primary, read all the verses in the upcoming primary lesson (the manual is available on LDS.org), and if there's still time afterward, sing the songs.

SING THE VERSES TO A TUNE

Pick a fun tune that everyone knows and try to sing the verse you are reading. Have the next person do the same with their verse. If you find one that really fits well, have everyone sing it together and memorize the verse using the tune.

You might find your children singing the roughly matched verses at random times. That's how children learn, so encourage it!

APP STUDY

If older children have mobile devices, have everyone download the same scripture app. There are scripture memorization apps, name-the-spot-I'm-reading apps, and many more. Find one everyone likes and have competitions or app-athons around the same scripture verse.

SIX DEGREES OF SEPARATION

Choose a verse of scripture and then randomly choose another verse. Work together to come up with six degrees of separation from one to the other.

Example:

> 1 Nephi 3:7 "And it came to pass that I, Nephi, said unto my father: I will go and do the things which the Lord hath commanded, for I know that the Lord giveth no commandments unto the children of men, save he shall prepare a way for them that they may accomplish the thing which he commandeth them."

and

> D&C 36:6 "Crying repentance, saying: Save yourselves from this untoward generation, and come forth out of the fire, hating even the garments spotted with the flesh."

Six degrees: 1 Nephi 3:7, Wilderness travel, Pioneer exodus, Fleeing persecution, Fleeing wickedness, D&C 36:6

FLOOR MAPS

If you're reading a war chapter, pile different colored blankets on the floor to represent the different landmasses mentioned in the verses (such as the river Sidon, Mt. Antipas, Zarahemla, etc.). Give the children sticks for swords. Have one child represent the Lamanites, and the other the Nephites. Read the verses and have them sword fight when the armies meet. Make sure they listen to the verses so they know who wins the battle and can act it out.

NOTES

1. See http://www.hasbro.com/common/instruct/risk.pdf for the official rules if you haven't played this before.
2. Richard G. Scott, "The Power of Scripture," *Ensign*, November 2011, 6–8.

CHAPTER 14

Which Methods Will Work Best for Me?

Some people might be excited about studying, but when they read all these methods, they won't know where to start. Here are some ideas that will help you choose which ones are right for you.

Once you've tried some of the methods on one list that matches your situation, try some on a different list. Use a method as long as it keeps your study of the scriptures fun and interesting.

I GET BORED EASILY

Name of Method	Page
Read on the Housetop	52
Social Network Question	72
The Old Hebrew Proverb	87
Add Illustrations to Your Scriptures	121

Share Verses on Social Media or Email	116
Play an LDS Trivia Game	118
Scripture Collage	119
Study While Doing Other Things	113
Book of Mormon Risk	126

I DON'T HAVE MUCH TIME

Name of Method	Page
Love Notes	48
Random Relatedness	47
Love Note Q&A	71
Find the Lord's Tender Mercies	89
Recite the Scriptures by Memory	92
Monologue Reading	109
Study While Doing Other Things	113
Share Verses on Social Media or Email	116
Shadow Read	117
Sing the Verses to a Tune	131
App Study	131

I'M A TEENAGER

Name of Method	Page
Look for Verses Relating to Your Life Situation	51
Do a Personality Profile on People in the Scriptures	58
Cross-Reference Your Patriarchal Blessing	57
Emulate a Scripture Hero	59
Create a Top-Ten Favorite Scriptures List	59
Study Your Interests and Hobbies	60
Social Network Question	72

SCRIPTURE STUDY *Made Awesome*

Study the Parables in Detail	77
Earn Your YW Medallion or Duty to God Award	99
Study the Bad Guys	105
Read a Movie	107
Reformat into Poetic Style	112
Rewrite the Verses into Rhyming Poetry	112
Share Verses on Social Media or Email	116
Play an LDS Trivia Game	118
Scripture Collage	119
Add Illustrations to Your Scriptures	121
Modernize the Parables	121
Scripture Study Soundtrack	121
Book of Mormon Game	125
Book of Mormon Risk	126
App Study	131

I'M A CHILD

Name of Method	Page
Quickly Draw What's Happening	108
Use Toys for Young Children	128
Switch Readers with Every Word	130
Sing the Verses to a Tune	131

I'M LEFT-BRAIN DOMINANT

Name of Method	Page
Study References from a Favorite Talk	43
Find Talks about a Scripture	43
If/Then	44
Color-Code the Footnotes	45
Study the Sunday School or Priesthood/RS Lesson	49

Chas HATHAWAY

Use the Bible Dictionary	49
Find Scriptural Lists	50
Read about the Savior for a Month	54
Cross-Reference Your Patriarchal Blessing	57
Footnote Study	80
Footnote the Scriptures	80
Create Your Own Topical Guide	81
Chronological New Testament Study	82
The McConkie Test	84
Look for Promises, Warnings, Doctrines, and Commandments	85
Create a "Teachings of" Collection	86
Scriptural People List	88
Scriptural Places List	88
Create a Scriptural Chronology	89
Go Highlight Happy	40
Study the Context	91
Recite the Scriptures by Memory	92
List Ten Scriptures by Value	92
Write Your Own Scriptural Commentary	93
Translate a Book of Scripture	95
Find Chiasmus	96
Look for Facts, Principles, and Doctrines	99
Word-by-Word Definition Study	99
What Is Different?	102
Verse by Verse Summary	104
Quickly Draw What's Happening	108
Map the Wars and Travels	110
Make a Labeled Diagram of the Scriptures	111
Shadow Read	117

SCRIPTURE STUDY *Made Awesome*

Bubble Diagrams	122
Scripture Trivia	127

I'M RIGHT-BRAIN DOMINANT

Name of Method	Page
Ask Why It Was Written	47
Whiteboard the Events as You Listen	47
Marathon 2: Listen to the Book of Mormon Once a Month for a Year	54
Marathon 3: Gospels in a Week	54
Listen to All the Conferences on LDS.org	55
Do a Personality Profile on People in the Scriptures	58
Create a Top-Ten Favorite Scriptures List	59
What Would I Do?	62
A & Q	70
Love Note Q&A	71
Play the "Why?" Game	73
Study the Parables in Detail	77
Search, Ponder, and Pray Cycle	78
Look for Know, Feel, Do	84
The Old Hebrew Proverb	87
Find the Lord's Tender Mercies	89
Scriptural Thankamony	93
Mentally Switch Roles	94
Write a Children's Version of the Scriptures	103
Read a Movie	107
Slowly Draw What's Happening	109
Monologue Reading	109
Reformat into Poetic Style	112
Rewrite the Verses into Rhyming Poetry	112

139

Study While Doing Other Things	113
Play an LDS Trivia Game	118
Scripture Collage	119
Study Hymnbook Scriptures	119
Name That Hymn	120
Write a Hymn	120
Add Illustrations to Your Scriptures	121
Read the Scriptures like a Melodrama	128
Use Toys for Young Children	128
Sing the Verses to a Tune	131
Six Degrees of Separation	132
Floor Maps	132

CHAPTER 15

When and How Long to Study

When and how long you study is entirely up to you. The brethren have made it clear that you should read your scriptures every day. Obviously, it's not always easy, but if you're creative and determined, it's definitely possible.

TIME OF DAY

Some people insist that the morning is the best time of day for scripture study. Their thoughts are fresher and clearer then, and there are less distractions.

But morning doesn't work for everyone. Many prefer reading at night after the duties of the day are behind them. They can sit and relax while they read.

More often than not, morning people prefer reading in the morning, and night people prefer reading at night.

And then there are those who find that the middle of the day is best for them, because they are more awake and alert. Sometimes work and school schedules make lunchtime or between classes the best time to study scriptures, and some parents find it easier when the children are all at school.

Don't feel guilty about which time you prefer to read. The point is that you read. For most people, maintaining a consistent time is crucial, so stick to whatever time works best for you. Be flexible if necessary, but make sure you continue to read every day.

TIMED STUDY

Another suggestion is to decide on a specific amount of time to read. It can be ten minutes or an hour. Only you know your schedule. If you choose to study in this way, try not to get distracted by other things. It's easy for fifteen minutes to slip away when there are bathroom breaks, snack breaks, respond-to-crying-baby breaks, and email/Facebook/Twitter breaks. You might read a total of three minutes with all the distractions that come your way, and it's hard to get much out of the scriptures in three minutes, especially if they are broken up by frequent "breaks."

Because of this, it's a good idea to be flexible and be able to go overtime. If the beeper goes off, it doesn't mean you *have* to stop. It just means you've hit your bare-minimum quota. See how long you can keep going!

I've found that the longer I study, the more effective it tends to be. For example, spending ten minutes fulfills the commitment to read and helps me keep the habit, but if I study for forty-five minutes, I usually don't want to stop, and by that time, my mind is racing, wanting to learn more. Any time I end my study period feeling this way, I am more likely to be excited to get started the next time.

A word of advice: if you are unable to avoid distractions and can't go over your time limit, this method of study might not be the most effective approach for you.

MEASURABLE READING

Another effective method is to study a certain amount of reading material at a time, such as a chapter or a page. This is good, because it means that no matter how fast or slow you read, you've accomplished a measurable amount of study. If you choose this approach, be flexible enough to continue if things are going well. Be willing to cross-reference and look up other sources. If you suddenly have a question that's not answered in the chapter, take the extra time to leave the chapter and answer your question. With measurable reading, it's easy to neglect some books, such as the Doctrine and Covenants and Pearl of Great Price, which are both powerhouses of doctrine, teachings, and promises. That's not to say we should give equal time to all of the standard works, but it's just something to be aware of with measurable reading.

I have a cousin who drifted from the Church

SCRIPTURE STUDY *Made Awesome*

during her teenage years. Despite her inactivity, she decided to continue to read one verse of scripture every night. That simple decision helped pull her through some difficult years until she was able to rekindle her testimony and come back to church. She says that reading one verse would sometimes stretch into a chapter, and then into a heart-felt prayer. She eventually returned to full activity and is now married in the temple.

There is power in the scriptures. In my cousin's words, "Even one verse a night can change the future of generations."

President Howard W. Hunter said the following about finding time to study the scriptures:

> Many find that the best time to study is in the morning after a night's rest has cleared the mind of the many cares that interrupt thought. Others prefer to study in the quiet hours after the work and worries of the day are over and brushed aside, thus ending the day with a peace and tranquillity that comes by communion with the scriptures.

> Perhaps what is more important than the hour of the day is that a regular time be set aside for study. It would be ideal if an hour could be spent each day; but if that much cannot be had, a half hour on a regular basis would result in substantial accomplishment. A quarter of an hour is little time, but it is surprising how much enlightenment and knowledge can be acquired in a subject so meaningful."[1]

STUDY UNTIL YOU FEEL THE SPIRIT

I once had a teacher who said, "I don't care if you read five minutes or just one verse. Your assignment is to read until you feel the Spirit every day."

At first I thought this was a cop-out, because if you're already feeling the Spirit when you get started, you might only read a single word and then put the scriptures away. But then I came to understand the deep wisdom in this approach. First of all, when you feel the Spirit, you *want* to read. It doesn't feel like an assignment or a duty. It becomes a hunger. Once I felt the Spirit, I couldn't stop, even though I was "allowed" to. And second, even when I was having a rotten day, no matter how bad I felt when I began my study, I always felt the Spirit by the time I had finished reading. That meant I was feeling the Spirit at least once a day, and that's a powerful opportunity. That year of seminary was a powerful year, and I believe that a big part of it was that I had the clear, unmistakable influence of the Spirit of God at least once a day.

In summary, I would highly recommend this approach. Just don't excuse yourself by pretending to feel the Spirit because you're in a good mood. Be honest with yourself. One way you can tell if you're feeling the Spirit is if you feel like studying the scriptures and praying.

That said, don't get depressed if you don't feel the Spirit every time you read. Most of us don't feel it every time. But if you choose this method and are persistent, you can become one of the few who always do.

NOTES

1. Howard W. Hunter, "Reading the Scriptures," *Ensign*, November 1979, 64.

CHAPTER 16

What's So Special about the Book of Mormon?

Many members of the Church use the Book of Mormon as their primary source of scripture study. This isn't just a general trend in Mormon culture. It's been encouraged by our prophets, starting with the prophet Joseph Smith Jr. Even in his day, members of the Church did not fully understand or appreciate the power and influence of the Book of Mormon. The Lord finally rebuked the Church collectively for treating the scriptures lightly. He told the entire membership that their neglect "brought the whole church under condemnation. And this condemnation resteth upon the children of Zion, even all" (D&C 84:55–56).

So that we might understand the seriousness of this problem, the Lord continued, "And they shall remain under this condemnation until they repent and remember the new covenant, even the Book of Mormon and the former commandments which I have given them, not only to say, but to do according to that which I have written" (D&C 84:57).

It's as if the Lord is saying that the entire church is in time-out, or on some kind of probation, until we remember and better follow the teachings in the Book of Mormon and other scriptures.

So what about us, two centuries later? Did this condemnation eventually wear off? President Benson, who was prophet only twenty years ago, quoted the above verse often and encouraged the saints to get out from under the condemnation that had plagued us for nearly two hundred years.

I asked a friend of mine, who is knowledgeable on this subject, "Do you think we're still under that condemnation?"

I believed my friend when he said, "I think President Benson helped get rid of that condemnation."

This made me feel much better—until I read this statement by President Benson:

> I do not know fully why God has preserved my life to this age, but I do know this: That for the present hour He has revealed to me the absolute need for us to move the Book of Mormon forward now in a marvelous manner . . .
>
> Moses never entered the promised land. Joseph Smith never saw Zion redeemed. Some of us may not live long enough to see the day when the Book of Mormon floods the earth and when the Lord lifts His condemnation. (See D&C 84:54–58.) But, God willing, I intend to spend all my remaining days in that glorious effort.[1]

Does this mean that all of President Benson's efforts to encourage people to study and live by the teachings of the Book of Mormon were in vain?

Of course not, but I believe we need to assume that we have a long way to go. I also believe that we must make it a personal and family effort to read the Book of Mormon on a daily basis and live by its teachings. It's not up to the

President of the Church to lift that condemnation in our own lives. It's up to us as individuals and families. According to President Benson, "There is no greater issue ever to confront mankind in modern times than this: Is the Book of Mormon the mind and will and voice of God to all men?"[2]

So, why is it so important that we study it? What's so special about it? What sets it apart from all other books?

At least part of the answer is in its subtitle: *Another Testament of Jesus Christ*. In fact, I would suggest that in some ways it's a more powerful testament of Jesus Christ than the New Testament. The Book of Mormon, in addition to testifying of Jesus Christ's actual presence and words (as in third Nephi and Ether chapter 12), also talks about how to develop a personal relationship with the Savior, how to exercise the Atonement in your life, and how to develop unwavering faith and trust in Him. It teaches profoundly personal principles that pivot on the life, teachings, and mission of the Savior, Jesus Christ.

Read the book carefully. The entire emphasis of the Book of Mormon prophets is to testify of Christ. The prophets who wrote it had no other objective. All their efforts to cry repentance were a determination to help us understand that without Jesus, we are *nothing*. Even while on fire (can you imagine?), Abinadi, in his dying words, included mourning for others who would suffer because they believed in the salvation of the Lord their God. And this, after years of declaring to the people that,

> Were it not for the redemption which he hath made for his people, which was prepared from the foundation of the world, I say unto you, were it not for this, all mankind must have perished. But behold, the bands of death shall be broken, and the Son reigneth, and hath power over the dead; therefore, he bringeth to pass the resurrection of the dead. (Mosiah 15:19–20)

That's no isolated Book of Mormon message. That's the bulk of what the Book of Mormon talks about, that Christ *will* come, that He *will* take upon Himself the transgressions of His people, and that He *will* bring about the great resurrection of all people.

Elder Bruce R. McConkie said that, "Few

men on earth, either in or out of the Church, have caught the vision of what the Book of Mormon is all about."[2]

Throughout your life, you will come across many people who will put the Book of Mormon on trial and pit it up against archeological findings, scientific discoveries, and intellectual philosophies. What they don't realize is that the Book of Mormon is not on trial—we are. God has never provided proof to force a testimony. He knows that if He did, it would only distract us from the faith, prayer, and personal guidance required to give scriptures their spiritual power.

The Book of Mormon is calculated to bring people to Christ—to bring *you* to Christ—and to strengthen your relationship with Him no matter how weak or strong it might be at the time.

This emphasis on the Book of Mormon, of course, doesn't mean we should completely neglect the other scriptures. Elder Richard G. Scott said,

> Do you use all of the standard works, including the Old Testament? I have found precious truths in the

> pages of the Old Testament that are key ingredients to the platform of truth that guides my life and acts as a resource when I try to share a gospel message with others. For that reason, I love the Old Testament. I find precious jewels of truth spread throughout its pages."[3]

I was baffled when I first read the Old Testament. Not only were there hundreds of stories I'd never heard, but most of them didn't seem to have any particular lesson in them. They were just . . . well . . . stories. But I was impressed with the Lord's constant guidance of the children of Israel. Even when they rebelled against Him, He still warned them and called them to repentance.

The first time I read the New Testament, however, I was deeply touched by the Savior's life and teachings. I had always known of Christ's kindness and love, but hearing the details of the healing, mercy, and forgiveness he showed was really special to me.

Because of my experience with the tapes, the Doctrine and Covenants was the first book of scripture I read. I loved the gentle guidance that the Lord provided to the early Church and the powerful and majestic voice with which He made his proclamations.

By the time I got to the Pearl of Great Price, I thought I knew most everything about the gospel. This book opened my eyes in a way that few things ever have. I discovered that despite its small size, it was packed so tightly with doctrine and the principles of eternity that it rivaled other scriptures in the amount of spiritual content. One thing I learned for sure: never underestimate the Pearl of Great Price.

If you're out of the study habit, focus on the Book of Mormon until your habit is restored. Once you've established a good, daily routine, begin diligent study of the other standard works as well. The scriptures have such a variety of richness that no matter how much you read, you'll always find a deeper level of knowledge and spirituality than you ever have before.

NOTES

1. Ezra Taft Benson, "Flooding the Earth with the Book of Mormon," *Ensign*, October 2005, 60–62.

2. Bruce R. McConkie, quoted in Ezra Taft Benson's "Flooding the Earth with the Book of Mormon," *Ensign*, October 2005, 60–62.
3. Richard G. Scott, "The Power of Scripture," *Ensign*, November 2011, 6–8.

CHAPTER 17

Family Study

Studying as a family can be a major challenge, but it can also be fun and rewarding. Obviously the ages of your children play a big part in how successful you are. If you have teens, they can take part in the actual studying, such as looking things up, cross-referencing, and contributing ideas. But if your children are under five years old, it's a different matter, because most children that age can't read yet. But that doesn't mean they can't participate. In fact, the younger they are when you start family scripture study, the more they'll demand it and the better they'll adjust as they get older.

Excuses to put off studying the scriptures as a family are plentiful, especially if you've done it a lot in the past. But the point is to continue doing it anyway, in spite of the excuses.

Newlyweds might put it off, saying, "We'll study when we have children."

New parents might hesitate because their children aren't old enough to understand.

Parents of toddlers might want to wait until their children have the attention span and the ability to not tear books and siblings apart.

Parents of preteens might have a lot of family activities going on and want to wait until their children have more time or are in seminary.

Parents of teens can't get their children to cooperate (when, on occasion, the children are home).

Some parents decide to wait to study until their children move out, since their children aren't interested anyway. And, unfortunately, empty nesters might put it off indefinitely, saying they don't feel a need for it since their children are no longer there.

I'm sure there are a billion other excuses we could come up with.

For most, having a regular time helps. Being

firm enough to maintain a schedule will help establish patterns of habit that will become easier with time.

Russell M. Nelson said,

> Years ago when our children were at home, they attended different grades in several schools. Their daddy had to be at the hospital no later than 7:00 in the morning. In family council we determined that our best time for scripture study was 6:00 a.m. At that hour our little ones were very sleepy but supportive. Occasionally we had to awaken one when a turn came to read. I would be less than honest with you if I conveyed the impression that our family scripture time was a howling success. Occasionally it was more howling than successful. But we did not give up.[1]

If you decide on a certain time to read every day, be flexible enough to work it into other times if you know the family cannot be around at the appointed time, and don't lose your scriptural momentum by allowing passing excuses to get in the way. It needs to be a firm priority or it will fail.

Elder Claudio R. M. Costa said,

> I remember when my son was seven years old. He was taking a shower one night during a storm when we lost the power in our home. My wife called to him and told him to hurry to finish his shower and to then take a candle and come slowly downstairs for our family prayer. She warned him to be careful to not drop the candle on the carpet because it could start a fire and the house could burn down. Several minutes later he came down the stairs struggling to hold the candle in one hand, and with his other arm he was carrying his scriptures. His mother asked him why he was bringing his scriptures. His answer to her was "Mom, if the house burns down, I must save my scriptures!" We knew that our efforts to help him to love the scriptures had been planted in his heart forever.[2]

At times when our family is really busy, my wife and I alternate between studying during dinner and studying while riding in the car. When we can't do it at either of these times, we end up reading scriptures as bedside stories.

Sometimes our study has involved a shouting match between the reader and a screaming baby. Clearly no one is getting anything out of the words being bellowed. At those times, Jenni and I remind ourselves that the most important thing is the habit—doing it at all costs. And believe it or not, it works. If only two studies out of a week turn out to be effective, that's two more than we would have had if we'd only made the attempt twice in a week. The secret is to hold family study every day so that at least a few of them are effective.

Also, if the children remember it as a family tradition and it matters to them enough (if only after many years of dreading it), then they will carry the tradition on to their families. What a wonderful legacy for your grandchildren, great-grandchildren, and all of your posterity ever after! You really can affect future generations by your determination now.

Elder Quentin L. Cook shared a great insight when he said,

> I hope we are reading the Book of Mormon with our children regularly. Persistence is the answer, and a sense of humor helps. It requires great effort from every family member every day, but it is worth the effort. Temporary setbacks are overshadowed by persistence. . . . We know that family scripture

study and family home evenings are not always perfect. Regardless of the challenges you face, do not become discouraged.[3]

The main point is to have it. Only you can decide as parents what to do to make it work in your home. You know your family better than anyone else—except God. Talk with your Father in Heaven. Tell Him how things are going and how you'd like things to be. He can help you accomplish your goals. He wants to help you, and He will. You just need to ask—and keep asking. Never give up!

NOTES

1. Russell M. Nelson, "Living by Scriptural Guidance," *Ensign*, November 2000, 16.

2. Claudio R. M. Costa, "Priesthood Responsibilities," *Ensign*, May 2009, 56.

3. Quentin L. Cook, "In Tune with the Music of Faith," *Ensign*, May 2012, 41–44.

CHAPTER 18

Scripture Study and Revelation

My favorite institute teacher compared the scriptures to an IV. When you go to the hospital for an operation or to have a baby, what's the first thing they do? They stick an IV in you. Why? So they have a route straight into your bloodstream. If they suddenly need to inject something into your body, such as a painkiller or an antibiotic, it immediately enters your bloodstream via the IV. You don't have to take a pill and wait for your digestive system to send it into your blood, because it's immediately there and can start helping you right away.

So how are the scriptures like an IV?

As my institute teacher Kendall Ayres was always saying, "Every time you open the scriptures under the right circumstances, you open a conduit to the heavens through which the Spirit of the Lord will flow."

I believe that, and apparently Elder Neal A. Maxwell did too. He said,

> In the revelations, the Lord speaks of how the voice of His spirit will be felt in our minds. He also says that if we read His words—meaning the scriptures—we will hear His voice. Many disciples have had private moments of pondering and reading the scriptures when the words came through in a clear, clarion way. We know Who it is who's speaking to us! We've all had the experience of going over a scripture many times without having it register. Then, all of a sudden, we're ready to receive it! We hear the voice of the Lord through His words.[1]

When you're studying the scriptures on a daily basis, you are connected to a spiritual IV. When the Lord needs to get a message to you quickly, you're ready to receive it. You might be at school, talking with friends, or in a cross-country match, but if the Lord needs to get His message to you immediately, He can do so. The act of regularly studying the scriptures keeps that line open.

Wouldn't it be awesome to converse with God the same way we converse with each other? What if we could send God an email and get a response like we would from a friend or a family member? Well, there's a way for us to get such direct communication. Elder Robert D. Hales said,

> What a glorious blessing! For when we want to speak to God, we pray. And when we want Him to speak to us, we search the scriptures; for His words are spoken through His prophets. He will then teach us as we listen to the promptings of the Holy Spirit.
>
> If you have not heard His voice speaking to you lately, return with new eyes and new ears to the scriptures.[2]

The messages God sends us through the scriptures won't always be in the words we're reading. Sometimes they come to us as random thoughts *while* we are studying.

At times while I'm studying I've found myself

being drawn to a certain subject over and over again. After catching my mind wandering to the same topic several times, I stop and think to myself, "Could the Lord be trying to give me inspiration?" I pray about it, and the answers come.

Regular daily scripture study will also help you recognize the difference between truth and the philosophies of men. So many deceptive doctrines encompass us, and without the light of the Spirit, we can easily be led astray. Studying the scriptures invites that light into our minds and hearts.

FISH PHILOSOPHY

Imagine you are a fish in a pond.

While in school, your teacher tries to convince you that it is impossible to see through water. Of course, this seems ridiculous to you at first, because you are seeing him through the water now, but then he stirs up the mud at the bottom of the pond. Soon the entire pond is completely clouded. You can't even see the other fish or the teacher.

SCRIPTURE STUDY *Made Awesome*

"See?" your teacher says. "You are in water and you cannot see. Now you know that it is impossible to see through water."

You and some of your classmates recognize that it is not water that is blocking your vision but the mud that makes it impossible to see. You recognize that when the mud settles, you will be able to see like normal, because the mud and water will again be separated.

But some of the fish begin to feel confused and lost. In panic, they turn to the teacher for help.

The teacher replies, "The only safe place is the bottom of the pond. At least there you can feel something beneath you."

They follow, because they don't know what else to do.

As the mud settles, they are buried in it. Their new perception of mud being the same as water is therefore confirmed in their minds, and they remain in the muck ever after.

Though unhappy in their new state, they pride themselves on their new understanding. They wonder how they could have ever been deluded into thinking that what they once experienced was sight. They scoff at the fish above, swimming happily about the pond. They mock them, telling them that their childish belief in "clear" water is just a tradition that their parents convinced them to believe. They say, "Yeah, we once thought as you do, but now we see what water really is. Sight is an illusion. You cannot trust your senses. The only safe place is the bottom of the pond."

Daily scripture study provides the spiritual insight necessary to tell the difference between the mud and the water.

The scriptures also help answer life's problems. Elder Dallin H. Oaks said,

> We often hear it said that the scriptures have the answers to all of our questions. Why is this so? It is not that the scriptures contain a specific answer to every question—even to every doctrinal question. We have continuing revelation in our Church because the scriptures do *not* have a specific answer to every possible question. We say that the scriptures contain the answers to every question because the scriptures can *lead* us to every answer.[3]

Scripture study is the key to the guidance of the Spirit, and it's also the key to overall spirituality. If you ever find yourself struggling spiritually, as if you are drifting or not in tune with the Spirit, immerse yourself in the scriptures. Look at them with new eyes, and the distance will narrow. God has promised that. He will guide you.

Personal revelation is an ongoing education. Every time I think I understand exactly how the Spirit speaks to me, He changes his approach. I don't think the Lord is trying to mess with me, He just wants me to understand Him better and learn every possible way that He might communicate with me.

Never get discouraged in your efforts to receive the Lord's guidance. If you're living worthy and *seeking* His guidance, He's providing it, one way or the other. If you don't have faith in your ability to hear and recognize answers to prayer, at least have faith in God's ability to reach you anyway. Read your scriptures, heed the words of the living prophets, fulfill your duties, and God won't let you go astray. He wants you to succeed more than you want it yourself. Trust Him. He knows what He's doing.

NOTES

1. Neal A. Maxwell, "Becoming a Disciple," *Ensign*, June 1996, 12.

2. Robert D. Hales, "Holy Scriptures: The Power of God unto Our Salvation," *Ensign*, November 2006, 24–27.

3. Oaks, Dallin H. "Studying the Scriptures." Unpublished Thanksgiving devotional to seminaries of Salt Lake and Davis Counties, November 24, 1985.

CONCLUSION

An Old Treasure

As you can imagine, my oldest set of scriptures is really thrashed—but it's a gold mine of study. It's the set I had through seminary, my mission, and my institute years. I have so many things marked in them that some of the pages might as well *not* be marked since no verse stands out above the others. The binding bulges from all the glued-in quotes, talks (yeah, entire talks), and stories. As a missionary and a student, I mastered the art of writing small, so in some margins there are more handwritten words than type-written scriptures. Pages have been taped back together, and the binding has been make-shift repaired many times over, so they're still holding together.

A few years back I received a new, leather-bound set of scriptures. I toyed many times with the idea of moving on to the new set. I even started taking them to church and using them for daily study. But I couldn't get used to them. It didn't help that I was moving quickly toward digital scriptures.

I kept my old set. I even transcribed the notes into my digital scriptures, rendering the old set obsolete. Still, they were something of an ancient treasure that I could never fully retire.

Then something happened that gave me new insight on those old pages.

I'd had a speaking engagement out of town, and knowing my phone's battery might die, I packed that old set of scriptures in my shoulder bag.

The speaking engagement was finished, and I was driving home along a seemingly endless desert highway when I saw a young hitch-hiker at the side of the road. It's not my tradition to pick up hitch-hikers. I lived too long in the city to ever fully convert to that. But we were in the middle of nowhere, and in small-town Utah, I thought I could at least give him a ride into town.

I pulled my car off the road and the young man got in. He was probably in his early twenties. He smelled like he'd been walking in the hot sun for a long time.

"Thanks," he said. "Not too many willing to help."

"Where you headed?" I asked, pulling back onto the road.

"The next town. I'm meeting my aunt and uncle there for a visit."

"No problem, just let me know where to stop."

We talked briefly about the weather, but mostly we were quiet. We were almost to his destination when he broke the silence and said, "Are you religious?"

I glanced at him. This was the kind of conversation I'd always hoped to have with a stranger but was too shy to initiate. "Yeah, I am."

"I have some questions," he said. "I have a brother who died at age thirteen. I don't go to church anymore. I guess I wonder why God would let that happen to my little brother. Now I feel like I'm too far from God to come back."

I nodded. "That must have been pretty tough. I do know that God loves you, and no matter how far you step away from Him, He's always only a step behind, waiting for you to turn to Him."

"Hmm. But what about my little brother?"

"That's a great question. I don't know the answer, but I know this life isn't all there is. Life continues after death, and your brother will continue to live on forever."

He considered my answer for a moment. "I wish I could get close to God again," he said. "I've got to start going back to church."

We were pulling up to his destination. I parked the car. "Do you have scriptures?"

"No. I should get some."

I considered the paperback Book of Mormon we kept in the side of the door for reading in the car, but something told me to pull that old set of

SCRIPTURE STUDY *Made Awesome*

scriptures out of my bag. They still fit comfortably in my hands.

"I'll tell you what. If you promise to read them, I'll give you this set."

"Oh, I promise. I need this in my life."

I handed him the set.

He thanked me, we shook hands, and he got out of the car.

I pulled my car back onto the highway. I didn't know this guy. I'd probably never see him again in my life, which meant I'd never see those old treasures again. But I wasn't sad. Something was right about it.

I'd spent countless hours with those scriptures, studying, underlining, writing in the margins, volunteering answers in seminary, looking up references in Sunday School, and reading from my roof or back porch after dark.

I'd also spent long hours reading them with investigators in Africa, perusing them by sunrise, and answering questions in them by candlelight.

Those scriptures carried me through the

years I served in, learned in, and finally graduated from institute. I'd read them with Jenni during our months of courtship and throughout our early years of marriage.

I'd given talks with only them for notes and had taught Gospel Doctrine class with them. I'd read stories from them to my children during family scripture study.

True, they'd become worn, and I'd adopted other scripture formats, but they'd been stalwart for so long. Only in the past few years had they begun to collect dust on the shelf.

I've heard it said that the best way to consecrate something is to give it away. Maybe that's what those scriptures needed. Maybe they were what the young man needed. Maybe they'll generate new life in him and walk him through an era of rebirth and revival.

But regardless of their destiny, those old scriptures are no longer mine. When it comes down to it, it's not about what I do with my scriptures. It's what the scriptures have done with me. In many ways, they have made me what I am.

SCRIPTURE STUDY *Made Awesome*

I testify that the scriptures are true. They hold the word of God and the key to His Spirit. Life is too short to neglect this priceless opportunity. Don't give up, and don't break your resolve to read them every day.

Make your scripture study awesome. Only *you* can do it!

And you *can* do it!

About the Author

Chas Hathaway loves living the gospel of Jesus Christ. One of his mottos is "If you're not having a great time living the gospel, then you're not doing it right," and he tries daily to live that way.

As a returned missionary, an eighth-year husband, a father of four children, and a Sunbeam teacher, Chas knows that it's in the day-to-day living of the teachings of the Savior that awesomeness happens.

ABOUT THE AUTHOR

Also a new age musician, an independent publisher of LDS music, and a champion whistler, Chas has written five original music albums and several arrangements of favorite hymns. If you ever start whistling a hymn in his presence, he'll immediately whistle in harmony.

Learn more about Chas at http://chashathaway.com.

Notes

Notes